ISBN 978-1-66640-525-5

Copyright © 2023 by Jurgen Ziewe

3rd Edition 2025

The right of Jurgen Ziewe to be identified as the Author of the work
has been asserted by him in accordance with the Copyright,
Design and Patents Act 1988. All rights reserved.
The copyright act prohibits the making of
copies of this work or of a substantial part of it. This includes making copies via
photocopying or similar process or via electronic means.

www.multidimensionalman.com

Elysium Unveiled - A Visual Odyssey of Life Eternal

How to read this book?	4
The Miracle of AI	6
The Vistas of Infinity	10
Near Earth Levels of the Astral World	14
We are the Creators	22
The Lower Astral Planes	24
Reality Dreams	30
People in Lower Astral Planes	32
Into the Darkness	36
Fear and the Dungeons of the Astral Planes	38
Demons, Monsters and Thought Forms	42
Places of Evil and their Inhabitants	44
Nightmares in the Astral Hells	50
Exhausted by Evil	52
Astral Helpers	56
Astral Workouts	58
Journeys into the Astral Highlands	60
The Highlands of Astral Planes	62
Astral Social Life and Amusement	64
Astral Adventures and Entertainment.	68
Astral Travels into the Unknown	70
Visiting Places and Re-enactments	72
Astral Heavens	74
Astral Villages	78
The Power of Creation	80
Astral Summer Lands	82
Astral Cities	84
Dream Dwellings	86
Cities of the Higher Astral	88
Exotic Places	92
Advanced Cultures	94
Dream Cities	98
Creations	100
Remote Dwellings	102
Places of Solitude	104
Astral Nature	106
Landscapes of Emotion	108
Underwater Cities	116
Underground Cultures and Species	118
Exploring Alien Worlds	120
Alien Civilisations	122
Alien Worlds	124
The Art of Manifestation	126
Higher Astral Heavens	128
Home Coming	136
Celestial Realms	138
Realms of Light	142
Realms of Beauty and Symmetry	144
Realms of Creation	146
Realms of Unconditional Love	150
Eternal Love	152
Celestial Bliss	154
Evolved Humans	158

When I had my first out-of-body experience fifty years ago, I unwittingly opened the door to a multidimensional universe. This life-changing event allowed me to transcend human boundaries, explore reality structures beyond words, and document my experiences as an explorer and artist. With advanced AI technology, I can now visually convey what words alone cannot describe, offering glimpses into what is known as The Afterlife and the vast realms of consciousness. Each image is a unique interpretation, inviting you to use your imagination. These visual representations are not documentary evidence but artistic recreations of states of consciousness. They aim to inspire and deepen your understanding of our inner world. As technology evolves, the convergence of physical and astral realities becomes a possibility. Through AI, I've strived to bridge the gap between our perceptions and the ineffable dimensions of reality. Remember that what you see here is one subjective view; each individual's journey is unique. As you explore these images, let your imagination take you on your own inner journey. Our inner worlds are vast and full of wonders waiting to be unlocked by our limitless potential. Embrace empathy and love, for they are the keys to harmonious interactions in the multilayered realms of existence. The images in this book are not literal depictions of the afterlife; they represent states of consciousness. Just as there are copies of Earth's physical reality on the Astral plane, each person's journey into the afterlife is a unique manifestation of their soul. Enjoy this journey, and remember that reality is far more than what meets the eye.

How to read this book?

Prepare to embark on a captivating odyssey that will take you beyond the boundaries of your everyday existence. As you delve into these pages, consider immersing yourself in a conscious dream, for the stories and visuals here are derived from a realm that transcends our waking reality. This is a world we all enter every night, only to lose its memory as we awaken to the familiar routines of our daily lives.

During the course of this narrative, set aside the mundane concerns of your working world and surrender to the authenticity of the journey presented. What you are about to read and see is a travelogue penned and illustrated by an individual who has ventured into this extraordinary realm for over half a century. He has dedicated hundreds of hours to exploring this domain, achieving a state of heightened awareness - a state we will all eventually embrace when our final day on Earth arrives.

Some individuals who have undergone near-death experiences feel compelled to document their encounters, often crafting entire volumes even if their time in that altered state lasted merely an hour. This compulsion stems from the profound vividness and authenticity of their experiences. In my case, having spent hundreds of hours in this heightened state of awareness, I claim the authority to share insights that extend far beyond the scope of a single event.

My journey involved not just a solitary brush with the otherworldly but a continuous exploration. I probed, researched, ventured, inquired, and even engaged in interviews with entities that inhabit this enigmatic realm. Above all, I forged a connection with the very source at the core of our existence, aiming to provide a testament to the intricate workings of our species and the multidimensional universe we call home.

So, as you navigate this book, embrace the sense of wonder and adventure that comes with traversing the uncharted territories of our consciousness. Let go of your preconceptions and allow your mind to embark on a journey that stretches the boundaries of imagination and comprehension. This is an invitation to explore the depths of existence itself, a chance to glimpse the profound mysteries that await us beyond the threshold of our ordinary perception.

Whatever can be imagined has the potential to become a solid reality within the infinite expanses of consciousness.

Every thought is a potential. Every idea is a reality in the making. Our minds are infinite, and so is the potential for consciousness to create and manifest worlds and universes we have no concept of. This is the unfathomable miracle of consciousness.

The Miracle of AI

As well as being an astral traveller, I am also a commercial illustrator, trained in using the tools of our modern technologies. However, using the latest artificial intelligence techniques allowed me to generate compelling and often photo-real visuals, which has been a profound bonus in making this book at all possible. For those unfamiliar with this revolutionary technology, let me put its main mechanics in a nutshell:

AI uses machine learning algorithms, specifically deep learning techniques, to create new artwork. The AI relies on verbal prompts and can also use visual prompts fed into the program, which is similar in many ways to a brief given by the client to a commercial artist like myself. The AI converts the prompts into images accessed and assembled from a vast database of billions of images, where they are mixed, reassembled and remitted together until they fulfil the original brief of the client. The AI is quite capable of "understanding" or better processing and interpreting even quite emotive prompts, such as "Love" or "scary atmosphere", "enchanting", "pretty", "exquisite", "morning light", etc., including quite technical prompts such as photographic aperture, camera type or even references to a particular style of representation and as the AI is challenged by its users it enhances more and more its machine learning algorithms. This way, it will continue to learn and expand its scope exponentially as new models of creativity evolve almost on a daily basis.

This level of sophistication allowed me, as the user, to rely on a vast repertoire of prompts for the AI to generate images that come close to what I carry in my memory and my imagination. Although it can require dozens of image generations to arrive at a specific result, it often happens with a level of accuracy that could easily be interpreted as "mind reading", and I sometimes wonder, as AI evolves exponentially day by day, whether one day the technology may be able to acquire a map of the artist's mind, based on tens of thousands of verbal prompts and tweaks, and quite naturally manifest the image carried within our memory which is close to our heart. After all, this is very much part of the manifestation process we employ when we cross over into the Astral plane when our time comes.

Our physical and astral realities appear to converge. We can already digitally visualise music in colour and form, which is a standard phenomenon on the Astral Plane when we listen to a concert. In good time we may utilise the creative astral powers via technological emulation to deal with the increasing challenges of our age with its compromised social and environmental challenges. But this would be looking further ahead.

In my case, the AI was trained to respond to my unique particular language via semantic prompts and specifications to the point of lyrical poetry to which I occasionally add my imaging style, derived from my more traditional work. When generating the brief for specific images required, I became increasingly aware of the kind of language the AI understands and prefers.

Feeding in hand-painted images as part of the process, adding to and refining the brief with verbal descriptions, the AI gradually arrived at an image close to my personal experience, memory and inner vision. In nearly every case, each image generated was twigged and fine-tuned over many generations of AI refinement, often leaving a trail of other images that were aesthetically very pleasing in their own right but not quite reaching the point where I

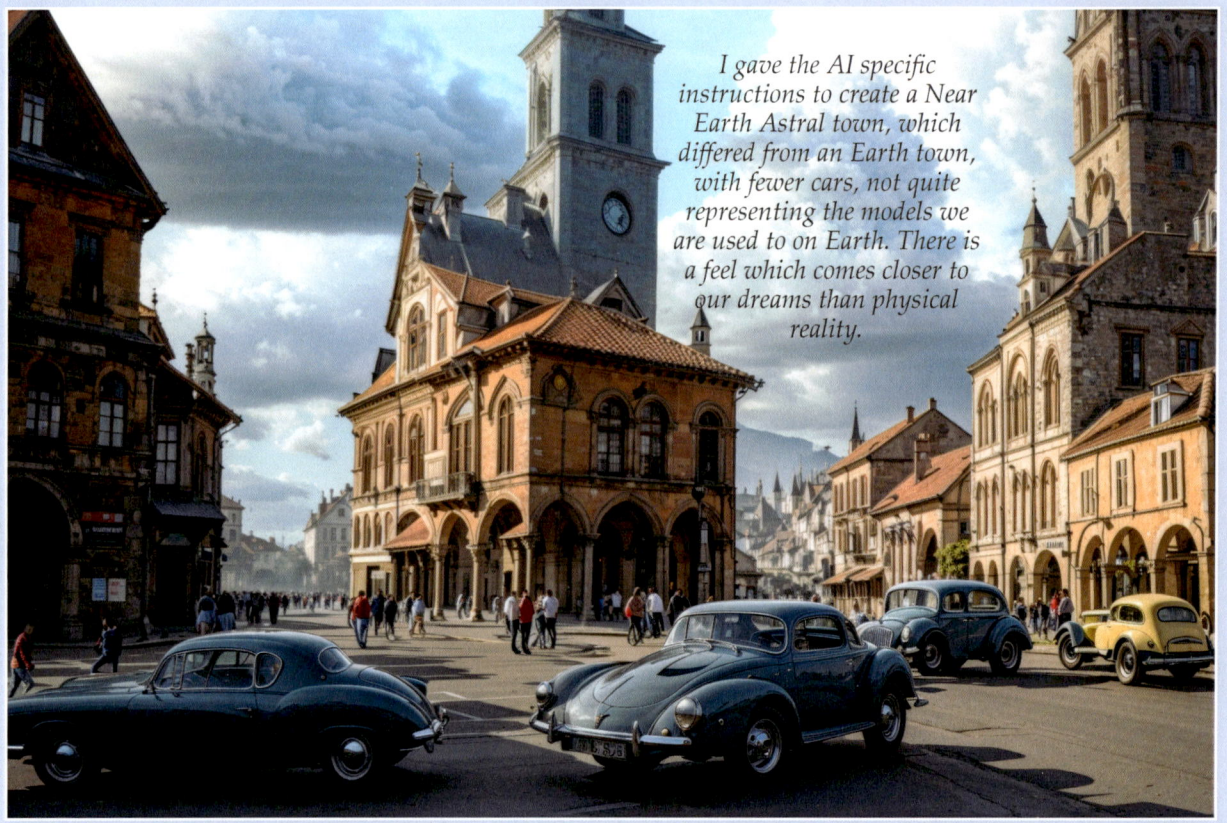

I gave the AI specific instructions to create a Near Earth Astral town, which differed from an Earth town, with fewer cars, not quite representing the models we are used to on Earth. There is a feel which comes closer to our dreams than physical reality.

"Earth II", as seasoned Astral travellers often refer to when trying to describe the world they frequently enter when out of body, is very similar to our Earth world which makes it difficult for them to decide whether they are actually Astral travelling or simple awake on some other place on Earth. Inconsistencies often alert them that they are no longer in the physical world.

The Miracle of AI

could say, "Yes, this is as close as I can possibly get to what I have seen and experienced."

However, there are still limitations which are hard, if not impossible, to reimagine even via the hand of the most talented artist who has ever lived, simply because aspects of higher dimensional life are hard to find words for. For example, how would I depict light that is "brighter than a million suns", which at the same time is a balm to your eyes, or colours that don't exist in our perceivable spectrum? Or sounds and melodies are so sublime to the ear that they would send you into ecstasy. The opposite also applies to the very dark negative realms where I encountered a chill unknown on earth because they carried torturous psychological specs unknown to us. All I was left with was shock and creating images that would send a chill down the spine. Nevertheless, I urge the reader to focus instead on the inspirational images later in the books and allow their imagination to be triggered by their uplifting quality rather than spending too much time on the negative. Images can be a trigger for meditation. So once you find an image that appeals to you, rest on it, close your eyes and observe where your inner awareness takes you while it expands on the visual stimulus. Sometimes this may take you on an inner journey where you will encounter new, unexpected environments and even events that are not of your own conscious making. This can be a form of meditation in itself.

Printed images have limitations our inner vision does not. Also, we are still talking about a technology in its infancy. At its present state, I also noticed that the AI struggled with refractions of light and subsurface light scattering when asked to create precious stones, for example, or specific metals such as car paint, or materials observed on the Astral Plane, which can not exist in our visible universe.

Sometimes the AI misunderstood terms with multiple meanings, and I was forced to resort to the Thesaurus to refine my brief by searching for fitting alternatives. Overall, some of these shortcomings were easily addressed manually, and sometimes the visual shortcuts it resorted to, such as representing people in the distance as stick figures, often added to the image's charm, which I did not feel needed correction. Being too literal can even distract from the quite unique atmosphere of the otherworldly dimensions, which the AI often contributes without my intention. On the whole, though, it is the miracle of modern AI technologies that enabled me to use multiple generations of instructions to unearth images which often enabled me miraculously to document content that I observed in the cosmos of the larger consciousness, which defied my skills even as an experienced commercial artist. It did so in the blink of an eye.

In my written work, I always emphasise how hard it is to convey experiences via words. So in this book, the medium of art is a welcome addition to deepen the impression of what is a uniquely subjective and personal experience. So use your own imagination when "reading" the images. Allow your imagination to take control and take you further into your own inner world of visualisation and

"Earth II" has an infinite number of locales, which vary greatly in character and appearance. They all have one thing in common. They are not quite what we are used to on Earth.

Astral travellers may find themselves in a sunny summery location, even in the middle of a cold winter. When they realise what has happened they often feel a powerful euphoria, excited by the prospect of unknown freedom of exploring a completely new reality and dimension. They can even call on their dead relatives.

9 *Elysium Unveiled*

The Vistas of Infinity

imagination because this is the world beyond our physical waking life. Allow yourself to be surprised and blessed by what may emerge. Open yourself to the wonders and miracles of your own inner world.

Nature has already blessed us with our imagination and our dreams, which, when turning lucid, will give us a glimpse of what is to come, a doorway into a far more expansive, wider world into which our limitless potential can unfold and progress until we get closer to the heart of God.

People often think that the Astral and spiritual planes are arranged in a stacked order from the lowest to the highest, which makes sense when considering reality in terms of frequency, but in nature, frequencies interlace each other and also interfere and influence each other which means at any one point, regardless of where or who we are, we can potentially transcend energies or descend from one bandwidth into the next. In this book, I will explain how the different frequencies and their corresponding environments manifest their distinct world. And rather than travelling from one world to the next, the only thing that is required is a change in the frequency of awareness, raising or lowering our energy, where raising means raising it towards love and clarity and lowering allowing emotions of various harmful kinds to take control of our awareness. Raising our awareness will enable us to move towards greater freedom, love, empathy and liberation, whereas lowering our awareness means surrendering our control and mainly assigning power to our base instincts and emotions, which can consist of a broad spectrum from simple attachment to profound bigotry, hatred and outright evil.

So accordingly, corresponding environments become lighter or darker, where darkness is associated with negative emotions, selfishness, ignorance, resentments, bigotry and others and lighter is related to clarity of mind, positive feelings, wisdom, compassion, heightened awareness and love. These more illuminated states

Trying to fathom or even approach the infinite Vistas of Consciousness with our human mind will forever be doomed to failure. The only thing we have at our disposal is consciousness itself, where our thinking mind can only provide a barrier in its exploration but never be able to supply an answer.

The only thing we have at our disposal is awareness and the experience of it, which may allow us to merge with its source and thereby come to know who we really are.

11 Elysium Unveiled

The Vistas of Infinity

also allow for more abundance, joy, symmetry and beauty, where emotions can be raised from contentment, comfort, and security into a state of profound bliss and even ecstasy, all of which respond with corresponding environments of beauty and symmetry, which I will try to express in my images.

The greatest mystery of reality lies in how individual souls synchronise to form consensus environments where they share worlds congruent with feelings and specific energy signatures. This happens on the shallow and most evolved consciousness strata. This is also the case here on Earth, where people congregate according to their social make-up, but on the more fluid energy levels of the spiritual planes, this is much more in evidence. They tune into consensus reality only when people synchronise at the same vibratory rate. These consensus realities create the different worlds and layers I have come to visit and endeavour to describe in this book. And yet, what you will find here will only be one of endless possibilities, corresponding to your own makeup and soul. The only way we will ever reach a common platform is via taking a position of empathy and love.

What I am illustrating in this book are not external places you may encounter when you travel on holiday to visit the Eiffel Tower or the Grand Canyon. These are only approximations, representations of states of consciousness and each one of us, when our time comes, will encounter our particular manifestation of our soul. This book does not provide "documentary evidence" or photographic "shots" from my journey into the Astral Worlds and beyond. They are artistic recreations and illustrations, though most important of all, I hope you will enjoy the journey.

Across time and diverse cultures, humans have harnessed the power of plants and mushrooms to transcend the confines of their ordinary consciousness. These botanical allies, often called "entheogenes," have played a pivotal role in spiritual and shamanic practices, enabling individuals to traverse realms hidden from the conventional waking mind. From the sacred ayahuasca brew in the Amazon rainforest to the psychedelic mushrooms of ancient Mesoamerica, these substances have been conduits to profound insights, mystical experiences, and heightened states of awareness. Alongside these plant-based journeys, practices like meditation and breath work have offered alternative pathways to explore the inner landscapes of the mind. Inner focus is the method used by the author. A lifetime practice of deep meditation led to the ability to induce Out-of-Body experiences and realise higher states of consciousness without using plant medicine or external agents.

13 Elysium Unveiled

Near Earth Levels of the Astral World

For everything that exists on Earth, there is a copy on the Astral plane. The most confusing thing for Astral travellers is to think they are in another location on Earth when out of their bodies. They are on an astral copy, though it may not be quite the same as on Earth. Sometimes, when they wake up from their Astral journey and sleepy-eyed get out of bed to get dressed, they find themselves again in another copy of the Astral Plane. Equally, when people die, they may find themselves in a copy of the physical plane and not realise that they have died.

This is confusing for many travellers and also confusing for the dead. They may wander around in a copy of Earth of what appears to be days and not realise where they are or what has happened until a kind helper, a relative or a friend who has gone before puts them right. However, they soon find out that things are not quite the same. Things they thought were familiar to them are different, even odd. Cars may not look how they used to, which may not instantly be obvious. Trains may be far wider or smaller than on earth, the streets and market squares may have hardly any traffic, some cars may have strange designs, taken from other eras, or there may be no cars at all. Buildings may look cobbled together or have overbearing architectural features, which would make no sense on our planet. Taxies may not look how we were used to, and some architecture may look more pompous and defy the rules of sensible planning we are so used to. The whole pace of life has changed; people

The Near Earth levels, or Earth-Two, feel very much the same, and under certain conditions, it's impossible to tell them apart, but things are not the same. Transport can be quite different, not adhering to the technology we are used to here. Buildings too may be quite odd and have their own particular style not easily attributable to an epoch.

14 *Elysium Unveiled*

One thing that becomes quite obvious to Astral travellers is that life proceeds at a much more leisurely pace than here on earth.

15 Elysium Unveiled

Near Earth Levels of the Astral World

may be malingering around, not at all in a hurry to go to work, or they may indulge in activities we consider absurd.

We are in the Astral counterparts of Europe's big cities. We find everything we are so used to, but ultimately, we know we are no longer on earth. Life has taken on a different colour, a different pace, and odd things begin to take place, odd things which would never happen here on earth. The way some people behave, their looks, their fashion, their social attitudes and behaviours. We have arrived in a society no longer fashioned by the social constraints and needs we know so well on earth.

These near-Earth levels are packed with people and are densely populated with earthly dreamers as well. They are freely mixing on these levels, the appearance of people doesn't change much either. They look as they did when they were still alive on Earth. That is part of the reason why so little seems to have changed here. It is often on this level where we meet with our departed loved ones during our dreams. It is only on the higher levels that people revert to their prime, looking young and attractive. Here, nothing has changed. I can always tell by this that I am on a level close to the earth.

Generally people here are not interested in anything other than what interests them, preoccupied with their individual concerns. Just like so many people on earth here too they look no further than fostering their self-interest. Their lives remain one-dimensional, conditioned by habit, often dull and mundane with little ambition. They are happy to maintain their status quo and not be bothered and are happy to be left in ignorance, which appears to be the focus of the vast majority of the population. To an awakened outsider, their lives appear dull. So they will carry on with their life in a state of unawareness just as they did when still alive on earth, trapped in a kind of sleep walking routine, like they always were without ever questioning the mystery of their existence. Eventually they "bore" themselves to sleep and then reincarnate without having sampled the delights of a higher, more refined state of consciousness. Others, on the verge of waking up, are beginning to feel trapped and wish to move on but don't know how. This is where they catch the attention of Astral helpers. It is as if they are waking up from a dream, which

16 Elysium Unveiled

The near-Earth levels are also the environments of human sleepers. An experienced astral traveller will recognise them by their somewhat dazed look. Other dreamers may act out their dreams here. Towns can be overcrowded, with people nestling or squeezing their spaces together, unbalancing the overall architectural integrity.

17 Elysium Unveiled

Near Earth Levels of the Astral World

was also a dream when they were still alive. They may ask questions and ready themselves for their onward journey or simply prepare themselves for another journey through the lower worlds of reincarnation, driven by an instinctive force they have no control over, which keeps them trapped for many cycles until experience gradually evolves their senses and they slowly awaken to their higher potential.

Of course, it doesn't have to be like that. Aspirations are powerful energies which can open interesting doors in this incredible world. In a world where inner feelings, thoughts and conditions so obviously manifest themselves in the outside world, this will inevitably have an effect on the attitudes of the individual, so it is quite natural that people begin to become aware of the quality of their feelings, emotions and thinking. I have noticed that people living here are generally more guarded in their thinking. Very early on in my travels I noticed reprimanding looks directed at me when I mentally judged a person I met. Thoughts come across like spoken words. So it is not surprising that people are more aware of the quality of their feelings, emotions and thoughts. Naturally, this leads to an aspect of self awareness and encourages a need for self-improvement. This in itself can set up a path towards self-actualisation and spiritual growth. This is one of the great benefits of astral life, initiating and accelerating our evolution. Generally, people begin to realise that focusing on heartfelt positive attitudes and selfless service will lead to more favourable conditions, and so they often, quite naturally, evolve into better circumstances.

Though a lifetime spent being rooted in self-centred conditioning and self-deception on our opaque Earth may find escaping hard from ingrained habits, so many people will persist in the personas they grew accustomed to. It is equally feasible that many I encountered on Earth-Two during my out-of-body journeys, who simply carried on with their old habits, it is equally feasible that many newly dead were unable or unwilling to adapt to their new condition as a result of unawareness. So they simply carry on with their Earth life as if nothing had changed. It was my encounter on these levels that motivated me the most to write my last book because I was dismayed to witness the static dullness and boredom of the lives of large sections of the world population, whether dead or alive, not accepting that new dynamics are awaiting them after they die. But of course, there are as many levels in the afterlife as there are shades of grey.

Talking of shades of grey, this is the predominant atmosphere on the many near-earth levels, greyness representing the dull unwillingness to embrace the new and change. Hence, these worlds reflect these states of mind, like murky November days stripped of the life and colour of spring and summer. It is clear to me that the lack of awareness of the living is largely responsible for the dullness of the near Earth-Two levels. Dead people getting trapped here often have no way of finding their way out, because the atmosphere and the consensus of the living is cemented into these strata so that many newly dead feel stuck here. Occasionally we see people standing out from the crowd, showing ambition and wanting more. Still, because these levels are largely a result of existential fear, anxiety and strive as well as an absence of love and creative joy, it amounts to very little. The consensus environments made up out of these kinds of widespread emotions is very powerful and so frequently new arrival remain trapped here, surrendering to the status quo, while maintaining

As well as encountering some very ancient forms of automotive transport, which perfectly reflected the atmosphere, I also saw vehicles which had no equivalent in our world, so strange that they triggered an extra level of alertness, enhancing my OBE experience.

There may not be much in terms of transport or cars, but what we find is often quite unique as cars don't roll off any production line. Transport can be quite non-functional as it is only designed to please the owner's individual taste.

Near Earth Levels of the Astral World

the same old social structures they were used to and conditioned by on earth.

Fellow astral travellers visiting "Earth-Two" consider this practically a continuation of Earth life, and it is hard to see any differences, although on closer inspection, there are plenty. But ignorance of those trapped here is wide-spread and the great benefit the afterlife has on offer is largely ignored. Sure, they naturally discover the gifts of manifestation, but this is simply a natural process of these energy strata, as are eating, drinking and breathing on earth. However, they are still rooted in an earth-like existence. Using flying as a form of locomotion requires elevated feeling, so people don't even think of it, let alone attempt it and are happy to trudge along walking as they were always used to.

There are taxis and public transport as they are here, even supermarkets, all consensus manifestations of the living as there is little need for purchasing food because it is no longer required to sustain a physical body. Nevertheless, old habits die hard. There are pubs and forms of entertainment, as there are businesses and shops, just as they are here, but the full abundance of astral entertainment we will find is reserved for the higher levels, the so-called Summer Lands. Here it is more a matter of "Why bother, we already have everything we need and want. We don't need to work to live, no need to worry about survival or health, and all is quite fine the way it is". So it is not surprising that many new arrivals will "pitch their proverbial tents" in these regions, simply because they don't know any better.

Like here on earth, there are many towns and cities, all different, but the prevailing atmosphere is one of the ordinary, the dull, the everyday. People go to offices without necessarily being productive. They visit pubs and cinemas, which never really reach the standard of our worldly pubs and cinemas. They use money which has no intrinsic value but is little more than tokens of appreciation or exchange. The only way people advance is by gradually realising that offering services and kind gestures to one another enhances their lives and quality of life. In this way, the creative power of love and kindness gradually emerges. When people become aware of these aspects of astral life and experience the benefits, their lives begin to open up. So professional service providers from Earth, taxi and bus drivers for example, begin to see larger benefits than simply earning money. Their service, in conjunction with kindness, earns far greater benefits than in the earthly past. Many people begin to realise the benefits of genuine service coming from the heart as their Astral lives improve. So we find builders, decorators, craft people, artists and musicians whose contribution to their fellow citizens brings benefits and gradually helps them progress on their journey toward higher, more evolved states of living.

We still find areas of poverty just as we find here, and charity work is ongoing. Still, it is focused on education rather than alleviating physical poverty because the poverty experienced is of the heart and the mind and can only be alleviated by the individual via a change of heart.

On the lowest near-Earth levels the atmosphere can be very dark and lifeless. Here we will find the "Lost Souls" wandering about, trying to find a way out of what is basically a state of depression.

The atmosphere changes from place to place. People are zoned together and attracted via similar states of consciousness. These states characterise the overall atmosphere, including the weather. A city here feels quite different than a city on Earth.

21 Elysium Unveiled

We are the Creators

There are major misconceptions amongst proponents of the Afterlife and life after death. The first one is the belief that we are here and the Astral Realm is somewhere over there, separated from us. The second one is that there is life after death when, in fact, there is only life. There is no before or after. Everything is happening here and in the now. We are constantly working on and creating the Astral plane while still alive, and our deceased loved ones are still as affected by us now they have moved on as they were when they were still around us on this physical focus level. We all share one consciousness, and the demarcation lines are only inside our heads. We are living with an epic illusion and delusion, thinking that there is a Now and After and a Here and Beyond. There is only a constant Now and a persistent Here. Thinking there is an Afterlife is still one of our greatest delusions, even among the stanchest believers in "Life After Death".

There are no strict demarcation lines between the states or levels of the Astral plane, but there are division lines between states of consciousness that clearly discriminate one from the other. For example, I could travel for miles through the dusky twilight of the lower region and then spot a luminous light in the distance, which turned out to be a town on a higher level of consciousness. Not everybody can even see it or be aware of its existence. If your consciousness is rooted in the negative, you may walk for many miles only to discover you have not moved much at all, but as soon as your heart and consciousness change, it will be like walking towards sunrise and with a bit of extra devotion and love towards a rising sun it may turn out to be a glorious city on a completely higher plane of existence. So what we see and experience is determined by our state of consciousness, and like here on Earth, we may never perceive the kindness of others towards us if we don't carry kindness within ourselves.

Nothing is guaranteed. People with a negative persuasion of character experience reality quite differently and may continuously fail in their quest for a better life. As heart and feelings are dimmed,

States of mind and soul are reflected in the environments. Regardless of how far you walk, you may never escape the poverty unless your heart and mind are changed.

Cities on the lower Astral levels can be brutal looking with large, intimidating concrete blocks, largely deserted. These are often the result of negative thought forms brought into existence by the resentment and negative attitudes of the inhabitants.

The Lower Astral Planes

In this environment, people cut themselves off to live in caves. Their bleak habitats are thought forms of negative energy rather than designed dwellings, however poor.

The dwelling on the lower Astral levels can be anything from subterranean caves to hovels in the desert. Nature barely exists, and if there are trees, they are leafless stumps. The environment is more likely littered with junk, which I identified as a junk of thoughts and negative emotions, wasted energy.

oriented towards the negative, focused on indulging in bigotry and resentment as well as other negative emotions or intent, the lower Astral realms quickly turn out to be distinctly more unpleasant, where people feel inclined that only a more determined focus on the negative will bring about the desired change, they can quickly spiral down into an abyss of darkness. We can also observe this process here on earth, where people become increasingly bitter after experiencing a setback, disappointment, injustice or betrayal.

Negativity here on the lower levels of the Astral can often be felt in the chill, which people try to get used to. It is cold, but it is a psychological cold, the chilliness of a cold heart. People living here in these heartless dimensions have no empathy for others and grow so used to this unpleasant condition that they become increasingly unpleasant. This vicious circle constitutes the dilemma of the lower regions and can spiral into something that our traditional religions describe as eternal hell and damnation. Though eternal, it is not. Like everywhere else in the Universe, nature is at work without exception, even in these dark and hellish realms. If salvation can not be found through a change of heart or the intervention of a benevolent friend or spirit entity, then exhaustion may lend a

I encountered a man living in a hovel that wasn't even large enough to stretch out in. I could see by his rather hostile look that his shabby dwelling was an expression of the poverty of his soul. Some people don't even muster any dwelling and just live in holes in the ground.

The Lower Astral Planes

helping hand. The exhaustion of negative energy may bring about tiredness, and the condemned person may slip into sleep and be transported through nature's mechanism and emerge in a new body on earth or some other dimension of reality where they may find a new angle to their future evolution as an individual soul. Here, they may start where they have left off or find a new connection via the inner mechanics of their soul to find an alternative angle to start a new life.

But until we get to this, let us spend more time in the regions of the astral level few would like to choose voluntarily to spend their time in. So what creates these environments that are so bleak that no self-respecting architect would consider bringing them into existence? The monstrous concrete buildings are devoid of love, without even windows, which intimidatingly overshadow whole regions of the astral environment with brutalist bleakness. When I first encountered these monstrosities in the lower astral world, I wondered what created them until I absorbed their inner energy. Their creation is simply a result of prevailing feelings and emotions of fear, anxiety, and the many offsprings of empty, disappointing lives devoid of any love and joy, an absence of meaning or any hope, full of despair and resignation. These are the architects behind such edifices, monuments of fear, worry, anxiety, and helplessness. Such energy has to go somewhere, and it finds its natural manifestation in such soulless, depressing buildings. Experienced Astral travellers can quickly sense their origin simply by touch.

I discovered monstrous thought forms built and solidified from collective negative energies. These were solid constructs, hard and immovable to the touch of their inhabitants, although I had no problem slicing through them with my bare hands and passing through them as if they were made of air. For the more permanent inhabitants here, this was not a possibility. The builders of these stark environments were the inhabitants themselves, aided by those still alive on our physical earth whose negativity lent a helping hand in their construction. It is worth considering at this point that our feelings and attitudes also contribute to the misery and suffering of those who have died and are tied to the lower worlds. So we find dilapidated houses with no windows in the lower regions, which are little more than ruins, are of our own making and the making of the departed and are the external manifestations of ruined, empty, fearful and selfish lives for which we share part of the responsibility.

Of course, on these astral levels, people still live in them. They have little choice because they resonate with the spirit that created them, but you can hardly call it lives. They are recognised as their homes as external manifestations of who they are and how they feel. They are like the monstrous brutalist buildings jutting into the grey-clouded sky I came across, advertising nothing less than the prevailing brutish atmosphere.

The sub-levels of the lower Astral planes are dark and cold places. The fires which manage to burn are often a sign of hope and when embers of warmth are beginning to light up, some inhabitants begin to learn there is hope for a better future.

On one of my excursions, I came across a group like this one, huddling around a fire. I was quickly besieged to take them with me, but I couldn't muster the power needed to lift them out of their pitiful state.

27 *Elysium Unveiled*

The Lower Astral Planes

So we begin to understand who built these massive, daunting and intimidating brick and concrete buildings. Their inhabitants are as poor in spirit as their habitats are as poor in comfort. What little possession they call their own is mostly worthless junk, like the quality of their thoughts and feelings. Nevertheless, they will guard it with the same jealousy and malice as they will guard their corrupted personalities.

An experienced Astral traveller, trained in the nature of consciousness during years of deep meditation and travels into higher states of our being, can see a little deeper and detect the nature and the origins of these thought forms. Although firm and hard to the touch for the people living here, these structures are nothing more than solidified thoughts for those grounded in a more aware state of consciousness. They can easily be penetrated, passed through or affected by visitors passing through from higher dimensions, seeing these obstacles for what they are, simply thoughts and emotions of no real substance, just like a trained psychoanalyst can see the connection between a client's state of mind related to their past experience.

An experienced spiritual traveller can ascertain and evaluate the often incredibly different and diverse environments they pass through simply by picking up on their atmosphere and the dormant energies and emotions that created them. However, they can do little to change them if they have acquired consensus status, meaning they are held in position and are maintained by a consensus collective state of consciousness. To illustrate, I have come across environments made of cardboard and precarious bridges which would crumble under your feet and immediately noticed what their mental origin was.

When travelling into the lower astral near-earth level, the predominant experience is one of pity and sadness and frequently a desire to help. These are the regions where Astral helpers are most active because these are states of mental and spiritual poverty, the equivalent to physical poverty we will find on Earth. They are here in these territories mainly because of ignorance, a lack of wisdom or insight into their own psychological nature. These people are here because they have learned to be here and often cannot move on alone. Astral travellers often take it upon themselves to help these people, sometimes at the cost for themselves of not moving higher into more lofty regions, and it is hard to find enjoyment in the face of such misery. Their enjoyment lies in the love and compassion they feel and the reward they earn when they succeed in transporting people towards the light. Here, we will often find people who themselves have earned their place on the highest spiritual planes but feel it is their duty to come here to help. They are the bodhisattva, the angels, the people who live in much higher states of consciousness.

Sometimes, in even very bleak environments, we see signs of hope emerging, like the rising sun breaking through the mist or colourful flowers spring up out of nowhere.

28 Elysium Unveiled

Nature on the sub levels of the lower Astral planes also reflects a prevailing mood which is expressed in the trees and landscape which may appear as "sad", with fog and the light dimmed, murky swamps instead of clear waters.

29 Elysium Unveiled

Reality Dreams

The sheer variety and diversity of the lower Astral realms are manifold and as complex as the diversity of negativity and corruption in our physical human spectrum. Every negativity and evil we may have heard about through history books or newspaper articles can be encountered here. Astral travellers easily pick up on the atmosphere of a place, even from a distance. They can read what is going on in any place instantly, like an open book. There are no secrets. When I entered some of these worlds, like the picture I tried to recreate on the far right, it became instantly obvious what energy created it just by looking at it from a distance. It was, to all intents and purposes, purported to be a hospice, at one point originally designed to help less fortunate people but became corrupted and turned over to be a hell hole of sheer evil, with the "nurses" in charge there to torment and torture their patients, who in turn did not possess a single shred of kindness in their soul.

You may now wonder what attracted me to such Godforsaken places. And I wondered about it myself, but I was not alone when I explored these places. I was accompanied by what I always referred to in my waking life as a "Silent Companion", a divine benevolent presence that accompanied me even into the darkest regions. I was surrounded by a benevolent shield of velvety love, which did not even leave me for one moment. I could see, but more often than not, I could not be seen by the inhabitants whose dour worlds I had descended into. For the energy of pity and compassion I may have felt, there were simply no takers, and I could do little more than to watch and to learn and only on occasion was able to leave a kernel of positive energy behind. I saw it manifesting in a dried-out dead branch of a tree, which momentarily would sprout a fresh leaf but very soon withered and died. But more often, there is little more to do than to wait until the negative energies have exhausted themselves. On another occasion, which I will document in my upcoming work, I was able to touch a soul and liberate it from its confinement. Though quite often, it is here that Astral helpers find their assignments.

Some places I have come across simply stand for nothing other than loneliness, desolation and emptiness. People in such a state of mind feel naturally attracted to this kind of environment.

People may share houses like the one I encountered on one excursion. The entrance floor was occupied by an authoritarian matron-like woman, who was little more than a tyrant who seemed to have everybody living in her house under iron control.

31 Elysium Unveiled

People in Lower Astral Planes

Poverty is a state of mind and emotion. The poverty of the soul does not mean people are condemned to these planes - quite the opposite. More often than not, reflection sets in, and it does not have to take long for people to naturally get closer to the core energy which nurtures them. People's external appearance and looks improve as their psychological state improves. In my own experience, I have found instances which take minutes from people evolving from what made them look like creatures from a zombie movie to pleasant-looking people who are transformed in their appearance by a change of heart.

People look poor and poverty-stricken. Their demeanour is mostly suspicion and hostility. If they don't trust each other, are suspicious, or show a lack of care it will be written all over them, not just in their facial expression but in their overall appearance.

32 Elysium Unveiled

33 Elysium Unveiled

People in Lower Astral Planes

34 *Elysium Unveiled*

Occasionally, I came across some monstrous structures, which I quickly identified as giant thought forms, summing up a consensus emotion on Earth, which related to a depressing news event shared by many people on Earth. In this case, it was a tragic car accident which involved several people and made the news headline.

Into the Darkness

Consciousness does not regard the subject of evil in terms of morality, what its causes are and what leads to it. It does not judge it in terms of right or wrong or who or what is to blame for it. It does neither condemn nor justify it. The greater consciousness simply regards it in terms of energy, evolution, randomness and entropy. There is no judgment, and what I will document in the following pages will deal with the outcomes of specific states of consciousness, decisions taken by individuals and the results and effects on the soul and their environments. Naturally, the reality of evil in our world can not be denied. We are confronted with it, if not in our personal lives, then via the media and the suffering people endure due to it. The injustices evil inflicts on victims and how reality finds its own way of balancing the resulting effects.

Naturally, most people are aware of the negative consequences of selfishness, with its extreme aspect of inflicting pain and injustices on others for self-empowerment and selfish gains. Society has made provisions for its avoidance via the laws and justice systems. Nevertheless, it exists even on a very private and personal level and even between people naturally close to each other. The repercussions will always be there, and some cultures refer to nature's dealing with such as Karma or nature's way of restoring balance and equilibrium.

People who embark on a spiritual path, setting out to live an ethical life of psychological hygiene, focusing on the heart and being mindful of the pitfalls of the lower mind are inevitably confronted with tests and challenges where they are forced to reevaluate their moral and spiritual integrity. Nobody can enter the source of their true origin still burdened with the attachments of the ego self, the flaws of greed, selfishness and negative attitudes. People will always be put to the test, if not on their inner spiritual journey, then certainly via challenges they will face physically.

Early in my exploration, I discovered caves or holes in the ground emitting an eery atmosphere. Only later did I find out that they were portholes in the darker realms of consciousness, serving as another form of metaphor we so often find in the realm of consciousness, granting us access to other realities.

On the lower Astral levels, we can find whole environments of dereliction, ruins and neglect, which are the appropriate thought form manifestations of humanity's neglect, indifference, ill will and fatalism. These kinds of environments also serve as habitations for people with similar mindsets.

37 Elysium Unveiled

Fear and the Dungeons of the Astral Planes

Having fear is the clearest indicator that we are still identified with the duality and uncertainties of the lower worlds. The moment we enter into unity consciousness, we become the sovereign rulers over our lives. Although we are still subject to the laws of the physical worlds, in the thought-sensitive region of the Astral realm, we are in charge when our identity is firmly rooted within the heart of a unified consciousness. That doesn't mean we are not tested or confronted with the negative energies of the lower worlds. I had plenty of opportunities to be challenged this way, which I have documented in my other books.

In the early days of my adventures into the Astral realm, I frequently found myself in true nightmare scenarios and wondered what corrupted part of my soul had lured me into these depraved regions. I soon found out that it was part and parcel of my spiritual training. Where my guiding force, which I referred to as my silent companion and I regarded as an aspect of a higher state of awareness, a kind of divine presence that had manifested in my life after a profound experience of cosmic consciousness in the early seventies, an experience referred to in my first book.

My descent into the abyss was a part of my training, and during some of my Astral journeys, they sometimes manifested in a way that would put the most gruesome horror movie to shame. Whenever this happened, I knew I had an opportunity to prove myself, to be reminded that my heart was anchored securely in the deeper consciousness of my soul. That doesn't mean I would not wake myself up into physical consciousness, drenched in sweat and valiantly trying to erase the experiences from my mind. I also learned that consciousness could not divorce itself from the sum total of its universal manifestation. Wherever we are, we are part of a cohesive whole, no matter how much we loathe the experience and try to get away from it. It is this that challenges the unfolding soul to enter these negative worlds to inject it with an element of love and salvation. For the spiritual traveller, there must be no fear left as they tread the path towards Unity Consciousness because, in the end, it is compassion and love that will illuminate the deepest recesses of human ignorance and suffering and assist in the evolution of the whole.

On occasion, during out-of-body experiences, I became fascinated by dark cave entrances on my astral wanderings through wide open country. Sometimes, they were located near a cliff edge. Some were holes in the ground or entrances into a dark mountain reached via a steep canyon. I can not explain the irresistible attraction I felt. It could have simply been that I could not resist leaving hidden places unexplored, wanting to discover what was lurking in the dark recesses of the tunnel network. In my waking life, I have always been fascinated by probing into my subconsciousness, exploring hidden fears and confronting any hangups. But here, during out-of-body experiences, they had a reality of a much greater order. They were physical, no longer theoretical concerns you could rationalise away.

Here, in their very physical reality, these environments were real, even more

Week after week I felt compelled to enter dark holes in the ground which emitted an eerie atmosphere. I needed to explore, not knowing what was awaiting me.

Underground and Hole-in-the-Ground phenomena are sometimes reported by people who had negative Near-Death experiences, where they fall or are lured into a dark abyss to be confronted by negative entities.

39 Elysium Unveiled

Fear and the Dungeons of the Astral Planes

real than real. I did not always have the courage to enter any deeper the moment I was greeted just by the first inkling of a menacing atmosphere, discouraging me from venturing any deeper. But it did not stop me. The pull of the unknown was too strong. I also recalled and realised that I had protection, and the lure of the unknown only strengthened my resolve to overcome resistance and venture deeper. On initial occasions, I just rushed through the tunnel network, ignoring the lurking entities nestling at almost every bend and with a sense of relief, emerged unscathed at the other exit of these tunnels.

In time I learned where they were located, and I bravely returned to confront my apprehension and fear. I discovered that, more often than not, my presence remained unnoticed, and with it, my confidence grew to explore in more detail. What didn't escape me was the revelation of the imprinted evil these subterranean catacombs harboured, imprinted like a gramophone record, in the walls and in the atmosphere, all kept alive and serving as the oxygen for their depraved inhabitants. It was simply a geographic entry point into a much lower, somewhat depraved dimension of the Astral world.

Most of the time, I remained invisible, holding on to my core state of being. Sometimes I tried to find weak spots or brittleness that were open to insert some positive energy or introduce an element of light so a transformation of energy could take root. More often than not, I was confronted with images of their horrifying, despicable past, so I quickly resorted to the fastest escape, even if it meant cutting my OBE short. In some cases, it led to me waking up sweaty in my physical body, not regretting at all that I had shortened my out-of-body experience.

Still, it was on these rather challenging excursions that I was able to ascertain so much information on the hellish Astral planes you may wish to skip over on the following pages.

In the early days as a novice astral traveller, when I hit these regions, I quite understandably emerged traumatised and shaken by what I had witnessed. I had no concept that such evil could even exist. If you watch movies about man's inhumanity to man, you may forget about it after a while, but on a few rare occasions, I was surrounded by it and quickly sought an exit. For weeks, I could not get these images out of my mind, and even now, forty years later, I still carry clear memories. When we have a nightmare that makes us sit upright in our beds at night, we slowly can pack it away as a bad dream. Still, if we are fully conscious and super aware, it is no longer a dream but a living experience and can leave a lasting impression just as physical trauma does. It is only when viewed in the context of our divine core consciousness that it loses its grip on us and is seen as a relatively weak force in comparison. I did not elaborate on these excursions into these underworlds in my previous books, and I had to learn to adhere to my source consciousness to be protected, detached and unaffected.

But to any Astral traveller, I would like to give a hint of warning not to enter or allow yourselves to be lured into these worlds if you do not have the superior power and protection of the spiritual traveller, with the umbilical cord connected to pure love. Without this connection, you can still fall victim to the complexes of lower mind psychology you must guard against. If you happen to stumble into these by accident, a heartfelt call to your guardian angel, your silent companion, helper or God will give you protection and cast a protecting aura or shield around you, which makes you unapproachable by evil.

When love is stifled and no longer allowed to be a guiding influence in life, fear begins to establish its anchors, and the ego tries to establish a level of control, and it does it by any means possible at its disposal. The more it loses its grip, the harder it struggles to assert control, even if it means the sacrifice of others or the suffering of millions. We have

The light I carried when descending into the abyss was mainly the light granted to me via my connection to my higher self, which served as a form of protection and could also render me invisible to others in these regions. However, on other occasions, I noticed that this light would illuminate the environment I travelled through for everyone to notice.

"Holes in the Ground" or "Cave Entrances" serve as metaphors for gateways into another dimension, like "Heaven's Gate" is a metaphor for entering the purely spiritual realms. They don't feel any less real than anything physical on earth.

Upon entering I didn't have to wait long before I was confronted with a tangible negative energy. They were "Black Spots" of energy, as we find black spots here on Earth, in some parts of our worldly communities - a powerful emanation and manifestations of a malignant energy with intent to do harm. Deep down, I knew this energy was limited, they were thought forms to me, and as such, were illusionary in nature, like everything that doesn't have a firm foundation in love and the clarity of source consciousness. So it could do me no harm.

Demons, Monsters and Thought Forms

seen it in the past, and we are seeing it now via the dictators and political demagogues operating at present using any means necessary. The outcome is more fear, and fear is an uncoordinated, chaotic energy, which is not pretty. It coalesces what energy it can muster from the frustration, the will to control and dominate to generate more fear-inducing thought forms to maintain control. The environments surrounding it are environments of fear and horror. Anybody unfortunate enough to fall into these pits will often not have the energy to free themselves unless they establish a firm connection to their source.

We may have come across such people in the news, in politics, in prisons, in the dark underworld of red-light districts, in the underworld of crime, slavery and exploitation, in the headlines of our media, and even in the bright daylight of everyday life, disguised as normal law-abiding people but morally corrupt. They can all be found in this hellish region because there is no other place with a corresponding energy. The only scant light coming forth is the energy generated by powerful negative emotions.

The people, if we can call that, are little more than freakish monsters because their god-given form has been distorted beyond recognition by the aberration of their minds and evil intent. Down here in the lower Astral, no fashion can disguise their true character. Clothed in dirty rags and dressed in the fleshy remnants of their ravished and emaciated souls, they fight amongst themselves for dominance and get the better of each other. Love is not a feeling they will have been familiar with, and such a word will only provoke scorn.

Without lingering in the abyss of such human depravity, we only have to look at the whole spectrum of the horror film genre of our movie industry to find out where the directors and screenwriters sourced their inspiration.

There are environmental manifestations on the Astral plane, which are the result of our indifference, lack of care, and ill feelings, and these create whole landscapes which are a perfect reflection of our consensus mind states here on earth and on the Astral Plane. Naturally, certain people are attracted to these regions because they reflect certain mindsets people are identified with.

Negative energy manifests in a variety of powerful thought forms, which, when sustained by their owner, can assume a life of their own, often haunting their owners.

People who are lost in their illusion, who have no other compass in life than their raw emotions of negativity, literally wander around in darkness. Regardless which level we are on, likeminded people will always find each other and flock together according to their mindsets, reinforcing their condition and illusion, their character and their emotional state of being.

43 Elysium Unveiled

Places of Evil and their Inhabitants

We will often find remnants of an epoch enshrined in the ruins of architecture where great evil and injustices have taken place. They leave the memory engraved in the environment and at the same time attract individuals who feel a synchronicity with such energy and choose such places as their haunting ground.

Being helpless, deprived of love and out of control often generates frustration and anger and the means to combat these shortfalls are often sought in more anger and hatred towards a perceived enemy. When the enemy is not another person, it is manifested energy of hatred which is solidified in monstrous thought forms. So a person afflicted like this will struggle against their own thought forms.

Our horror movies, reflecting our deepest fears are also reflecting actual realities on the negative Astral levels where real world horrors are not only recorded, but still enacted by entities who have totally succumbed to their most depraved emotions. Thankfully their victims are mostly their own thought forms.

Hatred against one another, which is quite prevalent in these depraved astral regions, often results in fights to the death, rendering the combatants into monsters. However, death is no longer an option. Instead, we may encounter severed limbs and even heads which are reassembled in tune with the fluctuations of prevailing energies.

47 Elysium Unveiled

Powerful feelings and emotions often generate self sustaining entities which roam around freely trying to attach themselves to a suitable host.

When rage and hatred are the cohesive power which binds groups together in the lower astral levels, they will always find enemies to oppose, to fight to the bitter end. Hatred is a powerful emotion; combined with bigotry, jealousy, prejudice, and racism, they create powerful thought forms which reflect their creators and turn them into actual monsters, as we can see in the picture on the right. Negative energy has an infectious aspect. We can see it in crowd rallies and lynch mobs during wars when the law breaks down, and the fever pitch of raw emotion sweeps along a crowd. Literally, a monster is unleashed over which an individual has no control.

48 Elysium Unveiled

Artificial entities are generated by uncontrolled and raw emotion and sustained by feelings of hatred. These entities can form complete viper's nests in specific but very rare localities if they are sustained and nurtured by their hosts.

Nightmares in the Astral Hells

In the hellish Astral regions, the mind is inseparable from the environment, and evil mindsets can generate not only corresponding environments but also artificial entities, thought forms which are prone to unleash their power on and attack their originator in a vicious circle, which is hard to escape.

Persistent hatred can evolve into powerful demonic thought forms, which frequently begin to control their owners rather than the other way round.

People of the same ilk soon find themselves appropriately clubbed together. These characters here have been nurturing a lifelong obsession of resentment, finding fault with the world and everybody but themselves. As their resentment never achieved any changes, they had nothing to offer but sorrow for themselves. They were drowning in self-pity, which manifested an appropriate environment in their afterlife.

Exhausted by Evil

Eventually, there comes a time when evil exhausts itself because its energy is limited. It leaves human wreckage behind, an exhausted and spent force without energy. Their minds are blank, and their hearts are empty. There is no enthusiasm or will left to confront their own faults and shortcomings in character. Very often, people like this sink into self-pity and despondency. They like to blame the outside world for their fate. They still find the fault in others rather than looking at themselves. Their upward journey has barely begun, but it is at this point that Astral helpers sometimes come forward to offer help and advice, which is mostly rejected and sneered at.

People who are devoid of human warmth or love and are filled with negative feelings of resentment and bigotry have these engraved in their appearance.

The quality of our character becomes quite apparent on the astral plane. There is no hiding from what we are on the inside. It will clearly manifest on the outside for all to see.

As the negative energy gradually exhausts itself and people show signs of resignation, the human features gradually reappear. They begin to look more normal. This is a time for self-reflection and an ideal opportunity for Astral Helpers to make their appearance.

A world devoid of love has very little to offer. It is a bleak place. Negativity is like a cancerous growth. It creates its own landscape of thought forms, mainly decay, erosion, chaos and destruction.

Astral Helpers

Where there is misery and suffering, there will always be kind souls ready to help. Their reward is the love and compassion they feel for the lost souls who have no means of escaping their predicament on their own accord and under their own steam. These helpers sometimes carry a light to attract attention, and those who are ready will call or seek them or even flock to them to find help or simply comfort. Of course, not all feel comfortable in their presence as the helper's purity of heart may often remind them of their own shortcomings, and they rather disappear into their familiar darkness. Light can be painful to those not accustomed to it. In the end, a person has to be ready to be helped and need to be primed for their own salvation. We often find Astral Travellers from Earth in these regions, referred to as "Retrievers", who made it their mission to take these stranded souls into the light. Some Earth mediums, too, can use their spiritual powers to guide people into the light. There is a great deal of unhappiness left behind to be dealt with by people who have died and have been unable to deal with their unresolved issues.

During one out-of-body experience, I was called to a house where a couple was going through a divorce. In my books and in interviews, I stated, "When we die, our internal world becomes our external reality." But this also applies

The distress of some newly dead people sometimes resembles that of mental illness. They are confused and unable to deal with unexpected astral phenomena, which materialise their fears and bring them out into the open. Astral helpers know how to deal with these common experiences, and sometimes, it only needs transmission of positive energy like love to restore peace and balance.

Astral Helpers go to places in the Afterlife attracted by calls for help and prayers. These distressed dead people cannot help themselves and are often confronted with Astral phenomena for which they have no explanation, which distresses them even more. These helpers, sometimes Astral travellers still alive on Earth, are using their own light and spiritual power to comfort and then lead these people out of these dark, confusing predicaments.

An Astral Helper carrying a light ignited by love

A group of Astral Helpers are attending to a new arrival trapped in a psychological crisis.

57 Elysium Unveiled

Astral Workouts

to how our emotional condition plays out on the invisible or Astral level. In this instance, the couple was still alive here, on earth, but in the process of splitting up. To any bystander on the Astral level, their conflict was clearly advertised for all to see and manifested in their material environment on the non-physical level.

The lady of the house put on a brave face, but it was clear by her appearance that she could not hide what she was feeling. When I followed her into the kitchen, I noticed that the floor had disintegrated into a bog. With every step, my feet sank up to my ankles into the ground. The woman felt trapped and in despair, which became apparent when I saw her sinking into the kitchen bog. As I approached to help her onto her feet, she broke down in tears. As I tried to comfort her, she collapsed into my arms and sobbed, shaking. I myself was close to tears and tried to console her as best as I could.

Momentarily I summoned some deep compassion and gave her to understand that the separation had to be completed, and she had to start working on the idea of a new start. With love pouring through my heart, I noticed that the floor became firmer, and she realised that my words had substance. I told her that, like the floor, her life would, in time, gain solid ground, and her new start would indicate that everything she was experiencing now was necessary for a completely new chapter in her life. She would be able to let go of the pain, and everything would, in time, return to a state of comfort and normality.

Astral helpers often escort stranded souls out of the dark regions into the light.

Sometimes, you can come across the Astral abodes of people who go through harrowing relationships or family crises during their physical lives. Although on their physical level, their house may be in immaculate order, even brimming with luxury and comfort, if the relationships are at odds, the astral counterpart of their abode can look the absolute opposite. I have come across houses which are literally falling apart, gaps in the wall or even the whole roof missing. Of course, if the relationships are worked on, the Astral house will also receive improvement.

Journeys into the Astral Highlands

It is a great relief to learn that the spectrum of the human condition is not confined to suffering and that tortured souls only represent a minuscule part of our experience as a human species. Still, there will always be those who will inflict suffering on others for their own selfish gain and gratification.

Most of our suffering is caused by the challenges encountered via our physical world limitations. The lack of money, sickness, being trapped in unbearable situations with no apparent way out and a million other challenges and frustrations are attributed to the restrictive laws of our physical world. Not everyone is equipped to deal with them wisely and harmoniously. This can result in mental instability, depression, mental illness, violent outbursts and even much worse. Being exposed to these challenges and learning to deal with them via the limitations imposed on us is a large part of the reason why we are here: to learn, to educate and to evolve as individuals and as collective souls. That is the reason for finding so much love and support from our spiritual helpers when we arrive in the Astral regions, which is frequently reported by people who had a near-death experience when they returned to their bodies to further their education.

That is why the far greater regions of human consciousness are spread lavishly over the infinite expanses of the vistas of creation, rooted in love, not fear or suffering. We are here to learn and to evolve towards our awakening into the clear light of our unity consciousness, towards love and into the abundance and joys of our eternal home. We are here to explore what it actually entails to be an evolving unit of consciousness.

60 *Elysium Unveiled*

We often hear how Astral travellers can be overwhelmed by some of the first impressions they may encounter when first arriving on the Astral level, because the feeling and the scenery can be quite unexpected and not at all what they had in mind. Changes in the atmosphere and realising that they are in an alternative world can often trigger a feeling of elation and excitement which unfortunately can also cut their experience short.

61 Elysium Unveiled

The Highlands of Astral Planes

Turning away from darkness, the aberrations of ignorance and blindness, which are largely the result of lack of insight, wisdom, love, and the absence of the many positive tools needed to lead a harmonious life, we can now rejoice and participate in the numerous reports of joyous freedoms and heavenly vistas so often reported by those who have moved across and then returned to their earthly bodies, with all the negative aspects of our corruptible human psyche laid to rest, which can cause so much pain and suffering. We can breathe a sigh of relief. Whereas before, in the dark realms of the Astral hells, people were trapped by their selfishness, a stubborn reliance on their bigotry, prejudice, their desire for revenge, or by deriving joy by inflicting pain on others, or simply being addicted to malignant and perverse compulsions to compensate for their perceived injustice, the lack of true fulfilment and true love. Here, we abundantly favour love, freedom and goodwill because we begin to realise that the base level of all reality is joy, love, creativity and freedom.

We are now on the verge of discovering our true heritage, reaping the knowledge and rewards along the way. In reality, we are already bathed in the radiant light of our origin; we just don't remember and instead search blindly for where it can never be found. Each of us already carries this light inside us. We are already potential light shiners. Here to cast light and love into the darkness of ignorance. We are challenged to discover, learn and unfold, but most of all, we are here to serve each other and the world we live in because this is where true beauty lies and unfolds, and with this attitude, our inside world becomes our outside reality.

From here on, each nuance of our thoughts and feelings will find expression and manifestation in our surroundings. We live in a dynamic universe where we constantly interchange with other energies surrounding us and where we naturally enter into the energy slipstream which is just made for us, where we share our world with sympathetic and like-minded souls, all here for the service of bringing joy and love into this world. To walk freely, unhindered, forever exploring and lending a helping hand simply because of the joy it brings.

Our worlds become brighter and more joyful. We begin to recognise that life is a blessing, not a chore, and with it, we begin to embrace and enjoy our new, more natural state. Being liberated from the limitations of the negative worlds and emotions, we begin to enter the infinite vistas of an expanding awareness. We witness what lies beyond the vast realms of our own creation. We learn new skills and experience aspects of a much more evolved life we didn't even know we were capable of. Our sensory awareness unfolds. We see, hear, taste and feel more clearly. The world around us becomes more vibrant and more beautiful, and we find ourselves in the company of people we are truly in tune with. We are just starting out, learning new powers and new forms of enjoyment.

Transitioning from the physical focus into a different environment of consciousness can be accompanied by trials and tribulations. Inevitably, equilibrium will be restored sooner or later, sometimes quite naturally, other times via friends, family or helpers. The world we may enter is a welcome antidote to our experience of life in the physical world.

63 Elysium Unveiled

Astral Social Life and Amusement

As a species, we certainly know how to enjoy ourselves, and on the Astral plane, there are new ways to enjoy. I had not one but numerous opportunities to observe how people were shapeshifting, transforming themselves by subtly changing their physical appearance from old to young, which is almost inevitable as part of passing over from the physical to the Astral level. It is also quite common, or better, quite natural, for people to change externally when their mood changes. We can see it here, of course, but not so dramatically. I noticed when artists were identifying with their subject while painting, they often took on features of the subject they were painting. I met people greeting me in dragon shape and then morphing into human shape with a smile. Interestingly I could still identify them as the people I knew. There is much fun to be had with this novel Astral ability which I reported on even on the very early explorations into the Astral world. I even tried it myself, turning into a dragon to see if I could. However, this kind of transformation performance needs focus and attention. If that is no longer maintained, people naturally slip back into the conditioned state they are used to. I recorded plenty of examples of this in my documented reports, such as the one illustrated here.

"What I was witnessing were not people in costumes but people who had morphed into fantasy animals, but they were not wearing masks of costumes. Their faces had morphed, and so had their skins. Inevitably every carnival has people on stilts, but these people had genuine long legs and arms, allowing for more exuberant expressions of their dance movements. There were dancing fantasy shapes, continuously changing, totally abstract and bearing little resemblance to the people who had transmuted into them. There were attractive alien creatures. People who had literally turned into dragons and now were flying through the air."

I was observing fascinating Carnival processions where there was no limit to how people were transforming their bodies, and I instantly learned where our desire to dress up came from. We are dynamic consciousness at the root of our being and potentially all creation.

Astral Social Life and Amusement

This simply illustrates that we have opened a treasure chest with these abilities which allow us to do things which before would have only been possible in our wildest imagination. People on Earth throughout history have always been fond of disguises or donning costumes, putting on plays, dancing, assuming characters to perform, and wearing masks. Personally, I always saw this as a memory from our nonphysical existence or faint memories of our many past lives where we assumed all kinds of characters playing different roles. That is why parties donning fantasy costumes are popular worldwide and in all cultures.

Once we return home on the Astral plane, we can express ourselves to our heart's content with liberty and freedom we would never have dreamed of. Added to this are our creative abilities, such as manifesting objects, sceneries and whole environments, especially in conjunction with others, helping to increase our manifesting abilities. We can even temporarily create living entities, which I referred to in my book and described as "artificial entities". These are not dissimilar from the demon thought forms emanating from malignant people on the sub-plane, but we are in control and not controlled by them.

67 Elysium Unveiled

Astral Adventures and Entertainment.

Can we control the elements? Yes, we can.

One of the most memorable experiences which I have documented in one of my books was what I referred to as the "Weather Show". These are public events where people manipulate the weather and the ocean with their thoughts, often in terms of a combined effort. It is common knowledge that people are fascinated by nature getting out of control, threatening our life and survival. We know of the storm chasers who risk their lives in pursuit of violent tornados. I myself, living near the sea, often find myself venturing out to the beach, rain, storm or thunder, to witness the spectacle of a storm surge. This twisted fascination of mine may have been the reason that I felt had drawn me to the "Weather Shows" manufactured by Astral Storm Chasers for the sheer entertainment of other Astral connoisseurs of nature's fury.

On one occasion, I recall the waves rolling in were towering way above our heads and knowing that I could not die, I allowed myself to be swept away until its energy was dispelled. The feeling was akin to being on a gigantic roller coaster.

It can be quite scary if people lose their composure and are taken over by an existential fear that often lurks within the deeper memory and comes to the surface, even though your rational mind keeps telling you that you cannot die. I experienced one such event during an astral journey where I was enjoying a calm swim in the sea when, gradually, the waves around me rose higher and higher until I felt trapped in a valley of waves and shouted out for help. As it turned out, it was my teacher coming to my rescue, revealing that he was testing my level of fear.

A recurring OBE experience which I enjoyed consistently was being near the astral counterparts of the seaside towns of Bournemouth or Brighton, where it was rumoured massive wave events would take place. The enjoyment consisted of riding these colossal giants without surfboards, triggering ecstatic experiences.

The Astral realm offers many trigger points, such as lights, bridges, and tall buildings. These serve as metaphors for affecting consciousness for elevation, transitioning to a higher vibratory rate or transformation.

Astral Travels into the Unknown

Many people are adventurers, explorers, investigators, researchers or obsessed with venturing into the unknown, even if it takes them to the brink of fear. There is little to fear on the Astral planes except fear itself, but there are plenty of opportunities to travel and pick from millions of unexplored worlds. People seek thrills in venturing into territories which are exclusively the domains of entities that are still fighting with their own demons. They may seek these territories out to see if they can be of help, try to satisfy their curiosity or confront their own inner demons. Or they may investigate subterranean kingdoms as I have, unsure of what they may encounter. I heavily relied on my intuition when venturing into the unknown. I could quickly detect negative energies radiating from specific places or entities, such as nature spirits hidden in the wild and remote areas of Astral nature.

Equally, you may discover with delight whole magical worlds completely reserved for non-human species, who control their own magical kingdom. On one occasion, I entered an expansive underground world of small nature spirits we may refer to in our folklore as dwarfs, which are not far removed from the ones illustrated in our folklore and modern blockbuster movies.

Astral environments offer challenges we will find nowhere else, connected with our most deep-rooted fears which we will have the chance to confront and resolve, similar to what can be experienced in Lucid Dreams, where we are able to conquer our most deep-rooted fears.

It is not unusual to come across cities and their city gates, which are overwhelming in their grandiose and epic scale. It becomes immediately apparent that the story and the history these features represent were at one time of great significance for the population.

Visiting Places and Re-enactments

"I was horrified to discover that I had entered a world populated by life-sized 3D cartoon characters milling around in a cartoon town. I was irritated considerably, thinking that I was still in some lucid dream state and tried to figure out a way of piercing this illusion to arrive at a consensus reality. I needed to be absolutely certain that this reality was not a mental projection or fantasy. But I wasn't. I was fully awake in another reality. After looking around, I spotted two guys with gamepad controllers waving at me and laughing. I discovered I had stumbled into a life-size game these guys had designed, a real-life Virtual Reality." (Vistas of Infinity)

After this experience, I realised there was no limit to what people could create in these dimensions. Any game the large game or movie companies could dream up was fair game for virtual reality exploitation but without having to don a Virtual reality headset. Most of the environments that already existed in the universal database have already been created and only needed to be called up and populated by real-life Gamers, fully immersed and a real-life fantasy world.

I discovered that anything was possible, and for days, my mind boggled with what could be achieved. We are only privy to a minuscule part of what consciousness is capable of when we are here and for very good reason. Here, we have to learn to overcome obstacles. Earth is an experience playground which severely limits our freedom and our potential for self-expression, at least in our physical reality, but not in our imagination.

72 *Elysium Unveiled*

Astral Heavens

As soon as we leave the near-earth level, not only will we be surprised by sceneries which are more vibrant and more colourful with new shades and hues we have never known on earth. We will encounter spectacular new kinds of vegetation, dramatic landscapes and completely new features, manifestations of energies we are totally unfamiliar with. The air is crisp and clear, as is the water, which instantly invigorates us when we dip in (and, of course, we can breathe underwater). Everything we encounter has its own unique energy. Let's touch a tree or pick up a flower. We can feel its intrinsic energy which communicates itself in various shifts in feeling, some so strange that we are completely unfamiliar with it, which instantly alerts us to the fact that in our earthly physical body, the range of feelings and emotions is vastly curtailed. An underlying spirit or consciousness connects everything, and nothing is really separated. So if we let go of the flower we had just picked, it will magically reappear in its old place. The grass we walk upon will feel soft like moss, but we barely leave an impression as we walk over it. Strolling through the astral lands will leave an invigorating feeling as we feel an intimate connection with the world. In a strange kind of way, we feel on home ground.

Nature on our Astral Heavens knows no decay but ever evolving profusion- driven to unfold continuously by its inherent creative forces

Astral Heavens

The aspects which cannot be described in pictures are that we feel more at home here than at any place we felt on Earth, which now appears like a distant memory, like an exile who has finally returned home after a long time away, rejuvenated, whole and healthy.

Wherever we go, we will be surprised by and come across things we have never seen before, landscapes with crystalline rocks made of semi-precious stone we have never come across or even considered possible. We are surprised by plants and flowers as tall as a small tree. Nature has thrown open a completely new catalogue of evolution. We find plants underwater and trees which defy gravity.

"I met a man who was nurturing some interesting trees. He told me that he grew his tree from scratch. Instead of branches, it had giant heart-shaped leafs. He said that the tree had a unique property which meant if you took a leaf from the tree, which was about a meter long, it would take you up into the air, and you don't have to use your own willpower and focus to fly. You would navigate with your feelings."

The feature-rich landscapes frequently has a human touch, like picturesque stairs carved into the rock, and wherever you rest, you can be sure you are surrounded by visual attractions, which seems to emerge naturally out of the landscape.

The incredible diversity of landscapes with new and unfamiliar features opens up new tapestries of emotions we never have and could not have experienced while still endowed with our gross physical bodies. Everything is energy in millions of shades of subtlety, from flowers on the ground, the mist hovering over the water to the cradling clouds in the sky.

Elysium Unveiled

Astral Villages

Villages and country life offered another new category of surprises. One that left a lasting impression was that of a small urban area where flowerbeds replaced the pavements you walked on without leaving a dent in the grass or breaking any stems. This was an unusual experience for me because not only did it feel good, like walking on moss, but the subtle energy of the flowers left a tingling pleasant sensation as I walked over them.

Flowers and meadows plays an important part in the life of the villages and small towns. In the country, I found that people mostly enjoyed leaving it to nature to do its random and beautiful design work. You could always count on variety and the fact that nature would dynamically respond to the mood and feelings of the inhabitants of the villages. I often found there was harmony as well as variety in the character of the villages.

Communal life is harmonious because people are naturally drawn together because they are on the same wavelengths. Every house has its own unique energy and aura, and by the subtle light it emits, I could often read something about the occupiers. I found this extremely revealing and a pleasure to study. There are no secrets because the energy radiated, or the auras are plain to see and to feel. This was much more enhanced than on the lower Astral levels.

Some villagers allowed nature free reign and even naturally encroached on their houses. Nature finds its way to generate diversity and often responds dynamically to the dwellers.

79 Elysium Unveiled

The Power of Creation

Architecture in the towns and villages can vary a lot but is usually style guided which makes a lot of sense because communities are created by congruity in states of consciousness, mind and leaning. Sometimes I was astounded by the elaborate carving of the exterior walls, the complex design and ornamentation, which is impossible on earth because time would never allow to make such extravagant and intricate carvings of large surfaces as here. There was never a shortage of plants and flowers either. Occasionally, I laughed out loud when walking along some exquisitely elaborate design. As I investigated it even closer, I found that the design had an inside of the design revealing even further and more elaborate detail. I wondered how that was even possible, which convinced me of the infinite power of creation on these miraculous dimensional levels. It was all brought about by thought.

I sometimes wondered whether these houses were created for decoration or as an expression of artistic design without serving the function of habitats, but I was wrong. I entered a house which was a three-story building. At the base, I met a shop owner who had some of the most beautiful collections of ceramics I had ever seen. Each pot or vase was made of a quality and elaborate glaze, which I could have spent ages studying and getting lost in their intricate design. I asked her if she lived in the house, and she told me that on the first floor, there lived two men together with a passion for model railways and that I was welcome to go inside and have a look. There was no barrier to entering their private domain as the woman seemed to be intimately connected to the pair who owned the flat.

On the first floor, I found the most fantastic model railway layout I had ever seen, running through several rooms. I was overwhelmed by the detail. Everything seemed real. Even the model trees looked like miniature real trees, but small.

81 Elysium Unveiled

Astral Summer Lands

The nature of our physical world, with its near-Earth Astral counterparts, is closely entwined with the emotional atmosphere of our earth level, is defined and shaped by limitations, stresses, existential needs, anxieties and dependencies on energy and food, shaped by poverty or wealth. The absence of these aspects makes for completely different environments. Environments now largely reflect pacified existential needs; this allows newly released energy to flow into the dwellings on the medium Astral planes. So we find luxurious hotels, palaces and multi-story dwellings, which would simply be featureless tower blocks on our earth plane. Shared or community living spaces enjoy a dramatic transformation released from physical restrictions such as space, cost, economy, transport, etc. It is easy to employ our imagination to understand what is feasible with our physical limitations gone.

We can sometimes find quite pompous houses occupied by people from another era who led significant lives on earth and have recreated their dwelling on the Astral plane. They may have been worthy and good people, perhaps living here with justifiable pride.

Astral Cities

Astral living serves a distinct evolutional and psychological function. The release from physical limitations and functional constraints also sets us free to deal with all our unfulfilled repressions and desires. For this reason, the Astral World has traditionally been referred to as the "Desire World" or even "Dream World" because all our dreams are increasingly being realised. However, we will notice that it is anything but a dream because our awareness and sensory experience are exponentially heightened as we unfold our potential and rise into higher states of consciousness.

Throughout their lives, people harbour secret wishes and desires, which largely determine the course of their history and fate because of the struggle imposed on individuals and society. Here, the released focus finds a new direction towards addressing unfulfilled desires, wishes and dreams. The prevailing energy and atmosphere allow us to access aesthetic beauty, physical and emotional fulfilment and comforts beyond anything we imagined possible while still tied to a physical body.

Big cities are also here; by "big", I mean big. We will find cities of any architectural style and epoch. There is no exception to the kinds of transport, from riding horses, bikes, cars or imaginative air transports. However, everything is determined by the astral region, very much as it is on Earth. Generally, there was much less traffic, but that depends on the region or Astral density level.

Naturally, all the benefits of traditional city life are offered here and more, with shops and shopping malls, venues for entertainment, market squares and street entertainment, which I described in detail in my other books.

Just like here on Earth urban planing is as much an aspect of city life as it is here. In my other book I described being part of a planning session.

85 Elysium Unveiled

Dream Dwellings

Here on Earth, houses, towns and cities are designed and built stone by stone, mainly serving an existential function: to shelter, provide warmth and protection against the elements, comfort, and, for a few rich people, an expression of their wealth and status. For most of us, it is simply the former.

When we enter the Astral levels, new ground rules for our habitats emerge gradually but increasingly dramatically, especially on the strata where creative energy is abundant, and the physical laws of nature no longer limit how we design our dwellings. Things that were impossible on earth now are only limited by the creative energy at the disposal of the builders and the power of imagination. Culturally, people are often still conditioned by their past and millennia of cultural conformity, but that gradually gives way as people discover that restrictions have been lifted. A new sense of freedom informs the creation of living spaces. The appreciation of beauty, symmetry and self-expression evolves naturally as people realise that the mind is the primary tool for creating living spaces, not conforming to physical limitations and money. Imagination is set free and liberated from traditional constraints. For example, we will find people's individual preferences manifested and realised to the full and to the extreme, like a completely white dwelling of luminous marble, with nothing left to chance. Of course, we will find it here on earth via the wish fulfilment dreams of the wealthy for whom money is no object, but here it is the ease with which it is achieved. A good example is the power of AI, which is increasingly used in art and which I rely on in this book, to conjure up images that closely follow what I have witnessed when travelling into the higher regions of the astral plains.

However, on the lower and medium Astral planes, society is still beset by restriction, not only because people still largely adhere to their conditioning, their tradition, style and fashion and what they are used to and comfortable with, but mainly because the free flow of energy needed for the building is still very much dependent on the prevailing state of consciousness and creative energy. So builders are still employed to construct because they have internalised their past skills and find it much easier to conjure up what is needed to create with the help of their passion. That equally applies to the other specialised skills and crafts we find on earth, from tailors to furniture makers to architects. Although acquiring new skills on these much more fluid refined energy levels is much easier, the population soon relies on the exchange, from tailors to glass blowers and any other specialised skill.

Once the architect, builder or artist has decided on the style of their dwelling, they will have set in motion energy currents which will assist in the building of their residence, attracting style elements from the universal database which naturally fold into the design, almost as if the house is growing like a plant. On lower dimensions, this is less in evidence.

87 Elysium Unveiled

Cities of the Higher Astral

In addition to this is the availability of total recall, which can call up skills we have acquired in previous incantations of in-between lives. For example, we may find we are perfect piano virtuosi and have access to skills which we totally deem impossible. People may find evidence for this skill recall in their dreams when they find they can play instruments or exploit abilities totally out of their comfort zone in waking life.

However, creative energy in the lower regions is much more challenging, and reliance on others for help is prevalent. The reward service offered to others is often enough to motivate people, which in turn helps their progress. Service soon becomes the mortar that ties the communities together, but that, in turn, depends on the prevailing energy of the plane we find ourselves in. There is little of this where people are generally motivated by selfishness and greed.

Our creative skills grow exponentially as we evolve through the Astral strata, increasing our energy and alignment to much higher powers. Not only do we have more creative energy at our disposal, but we can increasingly scoop from the wealth of data at our disposable via the universal information base, and we will find once we create a thought form of an object we wish to manifest, let's say a car, the energy released will automatically add further details by means of attraction we may not even have to think of such as a car engine. As I mentioned, we can also scoop from previous skills acquired in previous sessions of our former lives.

89 Elysium Unveiled

We reach a stage in consciousness where thought and manifestation become increasingly synonymous. This allows for incredible feats and miracles of architecture, which are as accessible as our imagination. We intuitively tune into a new natural flow of the prevailing atmosphere of a place, a culture and its people who were attracted to it. This allows for an overwhelming diversity of creation, which has no limits. We can travel from place to place and find completely new cultures of artistic and creative manifestation.

Of course, we find this on Earth when travelling from London to Venice, but it differs from what we will find here. Interestingly, this doesn't mean a free-for-all because the prevailing consciousness dictates what can and cannot be done via the laws of harmony, rhythm and synchronicity. An individual may try to experiment and break the persistent rules by creating a building starkly contrasting his neighbours. However, that doesn't last long; the architecture naturally aligns itself to the feeling tone of a place, and if they insist on carrying on with their intent of breaking the rules, they will naturally be drawn to spaces where this is not only possible but a guiding energy. So, what we refer to as building regulations here on Earth is regulated by the laws of harmony, synchronicity and beauty. We operate within specific spectrums of nature, where our imagination naturally follows prevailing energies. We find ourselves in an intimate alignment with our heart, which has chosen the perfect place of our new habitat quite naturally in the first place, including the community that forms our new circle of friends.

Because we are closely aligned with the prevailing state of consciousness via the intimate attraction of the heart, we will find ourselves in a position where we can almost grow houses and whole cities like plants, following the natural consensus within the community.

It is fascinating how a matrix evolves out of thin air. Visual patterns emerge first as thought forms, which gradually become more substantial, undergo changes as they grow, and, in the process, become solidified via a subtle energy of alignment and acceptance. So buildings, whole cities, parks and more, even landscapes, evolve and are grown in the astral nature like cultivated plants. However, these can not be changed in the wink of an eye by any individual because the moment people take ownership of the creation, they and their environment, in a sense, become stabilised and solid by the prevailing consensus.

I tested this out in one of my Astral travels when I tried to change an architectural feature at a fountain. Although I mastered the intended change, as soon as my attention withdrew, the element returned to its original manifested state. This is why these worlds are referred to as consensus realities, which differ from Lucid Dreams, where the individual is the master of the world as long as the individual dream world does not intersect with the consensus world.

"Growing buildings like plants" requires an alignment to a consensus and even the prevailing atmosphere and emotional energy, which sets up a distinct vibration and feeling tone within the given environment of the particular astral nature which cannot easily be overridden, in the same way as we would not build a boathouse in the desert. Here, we are required to align to a prevailing consensual atmosphere and symmetry to manifest our desires. Where this synchronicity is not given, we can move to a more synchronising environment on the vast and almost infinite expanse of the astral and spiritual dimension.

People naturally follow their inner compass and direction and intuitively feel guided by an inner calling, the unique melody or song of their particular strata of consciousness or soul.

Every invention which makes it's appearance in our world is first conceived of and prototyped in the higher states of our multidimensional universe, because our minds are rooted in the higher states of consciousness where creativity takes place.

Theme and entertainment parks are literally of another dimension with rides which would simply be inconceivable here, including novel experiences we can not even consider. One of the parks I visited stretched out for many square miles and even went underground.

91 Elysium Unveiled

Exotic Places

Sometimes it is possible to observe the emergence of new features and architecture right in front of our eyes.

93 Elysium Unveiled

Advanced Cultures

Imagine for a moment a world where the laws of physics no longer apply and are largely irrelevant, only perhaps playing a role in the memory of people in terms of nostalgia, of what they were used to in the distant past when they still walked the earth, concerned with their physical survival, their health and their habits and aware of a limited life span. They may hark back to the shortage of energy and material, the complexity and challenges needed to achieve specific outcomes. In some cases, this constitutes a powerful need for reincarnation.

Though more often than not, once people move from a two-bedroom flat into a sumptuous mansion, they waste little time dreaming about past poverties. We begin to get accustomed to living in a world that transcends all limitations. Like the AI I have chosen to conjure up the illustrations for this book, we are breaking the boundaries of imagination stuck in the constraints of a physical world.

Cities are no longer tied to trade routes because transport and locomotion can be instantaneous. I visited buildings many stories high but without staircases, and where they were still a feature, their only function was decoration. In my case, as I glided up the stairs,

One afternoon, during deep meditation, I came across what I would later describe as Thought City. A complex made out of various colourful domes, placed within the estuary within a beautiful park. It was like a university campus where every dome was dedicated to a different discipline.

Advanced Cultures

their steps changed colour and emitted musical tones. People design for harmony and aesthetic pleasure. They delight in aesthetically pleasing buildings, serve their enjoyment and taste and not serve a material function. I was fond of unusual spherical building styles with vast glass domes in various designs and colours, which would have been unthinkable on Earth simply because of costs.

It is easy to imagine societies emerging on radically different worlds that have little to do with our Earthy customs, styles and traditions. We hear so little about these societies on the higher strata of the astral planes because they have become so remote and detached from our pedestrian way of life and customs back here on Earth that there is little left that connects us. If we consider that life here on Earth with its vast, almost limitless expanse over the whole globe, let alone the sheer endless expansion of the physical universe surrounding it, then pit this against the infinite expansion in the astral realm, which is not even reliant on vast physical space but on consciousness itself on multiple dimensions.

Here on our relatively modest planet, we will need to think of ourselves as inhabiting the tip of an iceberg of universes that our minds alone will never encompass. If we already marvel at the fact that our Earth is only a grain of sand on the shores of our worldly oceans, we can not even begin to fathom what it is like to be a grain of sand in the multidimensional world of consciousness. We have nothing to compare. We can still travel through space in a sense, which I have done, passing through galaxies upon galaxies and skies upon skies, which were so alien that I could find no thoughts in my mind with which to describe what I saw because we are mainly dealing with consciousness where nothing is known.

It is not surprising, then, that we begin to embark on a path which opens possibilities which we can only appreciate once we have become accustomed via a step-by-step process of adjustment and readjustment. We will find that the billions of people presently occupying our planet and the billions who have passed on are well-catered in a world with no limitations. We are confronted with the tremendous unknowable mystery of reality and consciousness, and the sheer extravagance and abundance of it inevitably humbles anybody, even at the threshold.

The more elevated the dimensional strata, the closer they are related to the source consciousness the further they are removed from the constraints of our familiar Earth. Eventually, similarities to what we are used to become more remote. This is not surprising because the physical laws of Earth are primarily irrelevant. New cultures begin to emerge,

97 Elysium Unveiled

Dream Cities

evolving along completely different natural lines in dimensions that are so radically different from the physical and which have nothing to do with how we conduct our life here and in the past, and that includes an entirely new environment, which no longer conforms to any of our laws. The narrow bandwidth of our earthly constraints has given way to new parameters. The difference between the much higher strata and our old Earth becomes so different and radical that the past registers as little more than a dream from which we have awoken into a much more real and profound life. We will find very little that connects us anymore to the old. The people we left behind, perhaps? No, because we don't need to see or experience their bodies to be close to them. Closeness is an aspect of the heart.

99 Elysium Unveiled

Creations

When I went into these dimensions and wondered where my friends were, I immediately became aware of friends I had known many lifetimes ago, and they were still here. Not only that, but they were incredibly close to my heart in a profound, intimate and immediate way. Next, I observed one of my friends running through a field covered in an abundance of wildflowers and dressed in a flowery gown. We laughed and enjoyed that we were still so close, even though I had no link to her here on Earth or memory of her.

The environments here can be as straightforward or as complex as we wish. We can choose to live and frequent places. We only need to consider our wishes, and we will find them.

The miracle of the heightened state of consciousness is that our feelings, thoughts, and aspirations no longer discriminate between an outside or an inside world. We are here, and we are here now, and what pleases us is our command.

So let us explore in more detail some of the extraordinary features for our pleasure and entertainment to give us an idea of what is on offer.

People who wish to retire into the bosom of the spectacular scenery of outstanding beauty may choose a place of isolation perched on a cliff without consulting a structural engineer or a planning consultant. The place we choose and find is determined by mutual attraction. The site chooses us as much as we choose the area because both are attuned to the same energy. We

101 Elysium Unveiled

Remote Dwellings

may join whole communities with similar mindsets. Ultimately, we capitalise on our unique disposition and talents to enrich our particular culture, growing from our needs, likes and passions.

We can link up to our distant past, where we spend a happy time in a wholly alien and ancient civilisation, find our place there and even renew old associations with our friends from the past.

103 *Elysium Unveiled*

Places of Solitude

Earthly living is mostly compromised by limited resources. This is not the case on the Astral realms. Our living spaces have no limits and choices are as abundant as the universe. In my book "Multidimensional Man, I visited a community of people who decided to settle on a completely alien planet, where they designed a new life for themselves, unrestrained by cultural norms and restrictions.

104 Elysium Unveiled

105 Elysium Unveiled

Astral Nature

There are hundreds of testimonies of people who had a Near Death experience who reported on the incredible sceneries they encountered, which they inevitably described as Heaven because there is no comparison on earth. That is no exaggeration. What is much harder to convey are the feelings and the elated emotions that go with appreciating such sublime sceneries. The infinite expanses of landscapes change and unfold, continuously offering new surprises and the potential for adventures. The diversities of nature can be anything from snow-covered mountains, ancient forests, mountain sceneries made from precious stones or an idealised nature we appreciated from childhood. There are no limits.

It is not uncommon that we may find flowers the size of trees.

106 Elysium Unveiled

Occasionally landscape of outstanding beauty and interest are signposted with elaborate gates

107 Elysium Unveiled

Landscapes of Emotion

I learned early on that our emotional range here on the physical Earth is rather limited when compared to the vast and rich spectrum of emotional experiences to be had on the Astral level. It surprised me, first of all, how quickly emotions could be triggered, which brought feelings to the surface, which I didn't even know I was capable of. To me, it clearly indicated that our physical nervous system is rather limited in its scope of experience and feelings. But what was the most fascinating realisation of all is that every feeling we have there is on the Astral plane a corresponding environment into which we either emerge quite naturally and seamlessly or which manifests around us, initially as a thought form and then transports us there, but whether it is a place or simply a state of mind is impossible to tell.

This is the conundrum we find ourselves in when putting consciousness into a set framework as we do here. On this earth of ours, in this physical body, we can be happy or sad on the beach, in the park or in the privacy of our bedroom. Our environment does not change. However, if we pay attention when we are sad, even the sunset or the flowers we see look rather sad, perhaps to the point of mocking us, reinforcing our feelings. But in substance, nothing changes. On the other hand, when we experience or re-experience emotions on the Astral level, things around us can undergo dramatic changes. Suddenly, the world not only looks different but actually is different, and it is in keeping with our emotions. Our world is painted and "designed" by our emotions.

I first noticed this effect when travelling in flight through vast open countryside, and as my enjoyment of the experience increased, the hills and lakes I sailed over became more glorious, which enhanced my feelings of joy. Then, I remembered an event which was somewhat troublesome and which stirred an emotion of concern. The moment the emotion arose, the landscape around me changed. It started drizzling with fine rain, and I now sailed over ragged rock and yellowed grass. However, there was much more to it. Some features in the surroundings were a complete reflection of the nuances of feelings I had evoked. In this realm of consciousness, everything has a "feeling tone", fine nuances of emotions which cannot be described in words. They could appear as purple grass patches on a stretch of water reminiscent of a swamp.

The most fascinating aspect of this condition is that we can explore our feelings to their ultimate depth and origin as we travel along the landscapes of our feelings, where every aspect we pass has a feeling tone attached to it, which will reveal to us its origin. We may encounter extremely sublime spaces or aspects of our deepest concerns which will open to us like a book we can read.

109 Elysium Unveiled

Our most private and intimate feelings and emotions can lead us into sublime sceneries, perfect reflections of our feelings. We can explore our feelings as we travel along. We can enhance and transform them, and our environment will change accordingly.

We can travel through our emotions and feelings via a boat or allow the scenery around us to unfold and become aware of their deeper origin.

I often noticed symmetry and order in the landscapes I visited, as if nature, too, followed an inbuilt genetic rhythm.

113 Elysium Unveiled

114 Elysium Unveiled

Simply trusting our emotions and feelings with our heart can transport us into sublime territories of the soul because the moment we do so, the heart and our love become our guide and travel companion. We can completely surrender to it and observe where our heart will take us. A profound increase in joy will become apparent, leading us into sublime states of happiness and fulfilment and even guiding us to the celestial gate of our soul.

Underwater Cities

The first time I became aware that water on the Astral level was not an element that would impact my breathing was when I jumped into it for fun, like a clear stream. I instantly recognised its invigorating nature. Not only could I breathe freely as if I were breathing fresh air, but it was a completely new element of the Astral plane. Those of us who seek the pleasure of weightlessly diving and floating through a coral reef will have a powerful experience of this great and wonderful alien world we can experience. Just going snorkelling on our holiday in the Mediterranean during one beautiful summer holiday provided a glimpse into a completely different world, where you could glide weightlessly through unknown landscapes and mix with sea creatures of all kinds.

So it is unsurprising that some people who have taken ownership of their new freedoms on the Astral plane may decide to take up residence under the sea, if only temporarily, and build an aquatic dwelling that will give them a taste to mix with completely different intelligent species originating from a quite different line of evolution. In my previous books, I described how easy it is to communicate with animals and birds as if they were humans in an intelligent way. Just imagine the beauty and revelations to be aware of when we open communication channels between our species from a completely different line of evolution.

116 Elysium Unveiled

Within the Astral deep oceans and seas, we will encounter completely different species from another evolutionary chain to ours, who build their habitats here resembling coral reefs, but not less sumptuous than anything we can find on the human level.

117 Elysium Unveiled

Underground Cultures and Species

I only ever had a one-time opportunity to visit a non-human world, and it was purely by chance, a different line of evolution to our human species. A species which in our culture is attributed to nature spirits, like fairies, elves and the whole kingdom of creatures which so prominently feature in our children's literature and folklore. Even as a child, I was never interested in fairies and the like. I discarded these as fairytales arising as a literary fiction genre, and, as a result, I never had the slightest inclination to follow up on their validity during my out-of-body experiences. Even now, the topic is alien to me, and I never had the slightest interest in further investigating it.

However, it is easy to imagine the shock and surprise when I found myself catapulted during one Out-of-body state into a subterranean world that was populated with little people, no taller than a foot maximum. At the time, I was just aware, and I wasn't even sure whether anybody in this population knew my presence. Still, I could not help being fascinated by observing their ways and their culture, their way of life, their habitats and their marvellous and beautiful subterranean world, which was in some ways similar to our human world in other ways, at least culturally miles apart.

119 Elysium Unveiled

Exploring Alien Worlds

Until it happens to you, it is not real. Even after I started having out-of-body experiences, I looked at alien civilisations and reports about aliens with great scepticism. My first non-Earth experience happened when I visited some Astral counterparts of our solar system, of which Venus was the most notable and of which I retained the most vivid memories, mainly because of the sophisticated high culture and the unusual architectural design. The people I met there were distinctly humanoid and not alien. I think it is safe to assume that all the astral counterparts of the planets of our solar system, including their moons, are occupied by humans, but I cannot be hundred per cent sure. The first encounter I had with a distinct alien astral species was quite earth-like. Still, their appearance was non-human, with one eye planted in the centre of their forehead and a trunk-like mouthpiece, more what a child might imagine than a description coming out of the alien encounter community describing big-eyed Greys. I did mentally communicate with one of them, and he told me that their race was just as corrupt, dumb and uneducated as our human race. We both laughed, but that was the extent of my experience for years to come.

I did travel through what I clearly defined

The only way we will ever be able to encounter alien worlds is via Astral Travel and we can be assured we will hardly find environments hostile to our health. The laws of consciousness still apply, like attracts like.

120 *Elysium Unveiled*

Alien worlds and civilisations can naturally be so different to what we can know or even imagine that we have nothing to compare it with. The most striking thing is the "alien" energy and atmosphere, but it doesn't always have to be so different. I met an alien life form who confessed to me with a notable sense of humour, that his species is just as corrupt and ignorant as us humans.

121 Elysium Unveiled

Alien Civilisations

the outer space. I encountered massive space stations and ships. In my first book, I described a human settlement on another planet, and I visited planets with fascinating, completely new and alien vegetation and life forms. Nearly in every case, the beauty and otherness of their flora left me breathless.

It was much later on that I had an encounter with a very evolved alien culture who invited me onto their "space ship", which was nothing at all what you see in science fiction movies. The closest I can describe the means of transport were layers of energy, mostly white in colour, more like a flying carpet than a machine in our understanding. Still, that comparison doesn't serve very well either. Later, after visiting their planet, I became aware of why it was so difficult to identify their spacecraft. It had taken some time to make out the environment I was in on this completely alien civilisation. In "Vistas of Infinity", I described how I witnessed a sexual encounter of the species which could hardly be described as sexual in our understanding of the word, although it was distinctly erotic. Though without a visual reference, we would hardly associate it with eroticism in our culture, it was simply an outpouring and a unification of ecstatic love with visual representation which defied description.

I included some illustrations in this book which were purely the manifestation of the AI, to show that there is no limitation to what we may encounter when we have the opportunity to visit completely alien species. Anybody's imagination will be as good as the AI's or what we will find in Hollywood movies, which uses human species perceptual understanding to paint a picture. Still, we need to expand the limits of our cognitive and perceptual abilities a lot further, which may include the expansion of our consciousness to get a more truthful image of what an alien culture might imply.

This image is not an accurate representation of an alien world and only serves to illustrate that our multidimensional universe is infinite and anything that can be imagined is likely to have a manifestation somewhere. Consciousness is without limits.

123 Elysium Unveiled

Alien Worlds

The benevolent humanoid aliens who invited me to visit their world were incredibly handsome, with velvety glittery skin and dressed in a cloak which appeared to change colour as we communicated telepathically.

Alien worlds and civilisations can be so different from what we know down here that our awareness may require time to adjust and understand what it perceives and witness, because the energy is so strange that there are no ways to compare it with. At first I saw nothing at all, only an awareness of space until things gradually emerged and manifested into structures I had never seen before

The Art of Manifestation

As I described in my first book, "Multidimensional Man," there are a variety of forces at work when it comes to manifestation on the Astral plane. Mostly, we find manifestation is a subtle process which may not even be noticed unless we pay particular attention and, in nearly all instances, is quickly accepted as a normal, natural phenomenon, in the same way as we regard cause and effect on earth natural and normal, though here the cause and effects are thought and energy driven, which Astral inhabitants quickly grow used to.

Wanting a cup of tea is simply a habitual act of intent we don't even have to think about much. However, these processes are not as natural or intuitive on the much lower energy levels, where manifesting a cup of tea may be much more challenging and can even result in a cup of thin or tasteless tea or even worse. Positive energy plays its part, but how and what kind of energy leads to manifestation is a different matter, explained in more detail in my first book.

On the Astral plane, the process of manifestation plays a dominant part, and what we have seen so far in the book indicates what is possible and what can be accomplished. In some cases, active imagination can be observed when individuals or groups work to establish a scenery out of their vision. This creative process involves a give and take of working in conjunction with the natural forces active in the processing of thoughts via our awareness, which means we will have to work in conjunction with the laws of nature at work within our minds, very much in the way nature accomplishes plant grows on earth. It is a two-part process, an interaction between our will or intent and a letting go to allow nature to complete the manifestation process, a subtle interaction between two forces. Once we understand this process, true manifestation miracles become possible until we become true masters or even master magicians. We only have to look at the performances of our earthly gymnasts and the acrobatic feats they can accomplish simply as a result of years of practice and training. The same can be said about people spending years and years in meditation until they can achieve real feats of consciousness like having OBEs or controlling their dreams, healing or accomplishing remote viewing.

Consciousness is our greatest mystery, the greatest miracle of life, the processes of nature, and the universe behind it. We only have to look at the miracle of our birth, where we start being smaller than the width of a hair and then grow into adulthood as thinking and functioning human beings. How miraculous is that? Miracles happen every second we are alive here, and we are mostly unaware of it.

127 Elysium Unveiled

Higher Astral Heavens

It is rare while still alive in this dense physical world of ours to experience sustained happiness. Happiness is usually curtailed to specific events; even then, they are short-lived. I often wonder why this may be why people so often resort to drugs, lacking the psychological or material means to find comfort, let alone happiness, in their lives. So it is unsurprising that the near-earth levels appear so crowded when people die because this state of consciousness is what people generally are most familiar with.

So what are the psychological prerequisites to take us into the Astral "Summer Land" or, further still, into the "Astral Heavens"? First and foremost, we will have overcome our attachments to negative mindsets and become used to leading a life of psychological hygiene. That means living life through the heart, a life of care, paying attention to others, a life of love and appreciation. Appreciation and gratitude are the most important faculties to nurture while still on earth to get our passport into Heaven.

We often find here on earth the most contented and happy people are those who dedicate their lives to helping others, enriching their lives and empowering them while doing so with devotion, care and honest compassion rather than as a result of duty or for payment. Ironically, people who are so inclined will often be found doing charitable work in the lower or near earth regions, where they are needed most. Still, their home is in the Astral Heaven, where they recharge, mix socially with friends, drink from the eternal fountains of youth and wisdom and plot their voyage through the eternal life before them.

When we visit these realms, we soon learn how rich, varied and beautiful these environments are. The most noticeable feeling is the feeling of belonging, of being home and among good friends whose presence richly enhances our feelings of happiness and good fortune. There is not a single aspect of our life that is not greatly enhanced. For a start, our sensory perceptions are so vastly enriched

129 Elysium Unveiled

Higher Astral Heavens

that we may feel drunk with their pleasure. We have woken up from a dream, and for the first time, we feel this is where we truly belong. We are home at last. Our earth life appears like a distant bad dream from which we have awoken. What is more, we find ourselves reunited with the loved ones we so sorely missed when they exited our lives before us in such a painful way. The loneliness we have felt is no longer there, and a completely new life is opening up before us.

Humans are social animals, and we thrive best in the community and company of others, and that is what we will find enhanced in a dimension and in a way we could not have imagined. Our communal spaces are enriched and varied. In my other books, I described ten-star hotels and places of entertainment that are impossible even to envisage. Here on earth, only the wealthiest have access to the luxuries of an abundant lifestyle, but here, we only have to be rich of heart to receive such pleasures.

Let us linger in the towns situated within beautiful parks and landscapes and take in the soft and mellow light and its heart warming atmosphere. The light is a blanket for our soul, which changes according to the depth level of our appreciation. Atmospheres are something we have become much more aware of. The slightest nuances of feelings are registered and shared. The environment has aspects of sound we have never heard, where we discover that the murmuring brook with its tiny waterfall composes a melody of musical notes rather than delivers the white noise of rushing water we were so used to on our old earth. Yes, and the birds in this heavenly paradise sing songs we like to hear and appreciate, and they talk to us and celebrate the glory of this enchanting world.

Moreover, we discover new aspects we could not even dream of. There are beautiful sceneries here on earth which, because of their outstanding natural beauty, attract thousands of visitors every year. We find these here as well, but

131 Elysium Unveiled

Higher Astral Heavens

the sceneries have an added dimension of scale, grandeur and beauty. We are simply awestruck and rendered silent.

Then, there are completely new aspects and wonders of nature we can not even imagine. On the medium Astral levels, I found extensive amusement parks with attractions which would put our earthly Disney Lands to shame. Still, here, nature provides attractions that put everything on an extra dimension: vast caves, mountains, glorious islands, flora and fauna, which will render us breathless and people creating architectures beyond any scope and scale we could have imagined.

Festivities are in abundance. The joyful atmosphere radiates over the whole area and we can witness it visually, because the music, sounds and feeling manifest in ever-changing beautiful aura pattern over the whole regions which can be seen and felt from the distance.

133 Elysium Unveiled

Architectural styles and designs are not strictly subject to planning restriction. They are more dictated by prevailing consensus taste and atmosphere. Nevertheless, planning departments exist as they do here in our world, where creative people get together to pool their creative minds, while not everything is subject to control, allowing for a degree of freedom.

Home Coming

Before we leave the physical reality, we must consider why we are here in the first place and that this hard, resistant reality allows us to develop powers and characteristics unavailable to us in any other of the dynamic non-physical realities, namely the acquisition of willpower. We live in a world of resistance on earth. Nowhere else will we have such great opportunities to develop these characteristics of overcoming adversity by acquiring this particular kind of strength. The fact that so many of us are now emerging from the confinements of the material world, points to the fact that humanity is on a path to integrate these two extremes, the unity consciousness with the experience of separation.

When I had another profound experience of singularity during a mountain retreat in 2013, experiencing the great clarity of Unity, I was left with the overwhelming impression that there was nothing at all to it, that every single person on earth had potentially the opportunity to "awaken" to their singular Consciousness, which in essence is nothing more than a matter of recall, because singularity is already our base state of Consciousness and everything else in our lives is simply a distrac-

137 Elysium Unveiled

Celestial Realms

tion from the truth. This veil must be moved to one side to allow our full integration as a self-realised soul.

It seems that the veil and our distractions, which allowed us to get lost and confused in the labyrinth of such solid physical experience, are the root cause which prevents us from realising the profound state of our Unity Consciousness. People find an excuse for their distraction by claiming that it is more important to be here in the physical world with our ego unquestioningly engaged in meeting our challenges than floating around in some celestial heaven, in a perceived empty state of perpetual bliss. This, to me, is a complete misunderstanding of our base consciousness and a clear indicator of how difficult it is to convey the true meaning of Unity Consciousness to those firmly identified with their three-dimensional ego state. This is quite understandable. Unity Consciousness is our core state, our

138 *Elysium Unveiled*

Stairway to Heaven

139 Elysium Unveiled

Celestial Realms

home state towards which we are evolving quite naturally and, in the process, open up our cognitive and spiritual skill sets, our heart, our wisdom, our compassion and our understanding, which in turn will help us integrate our physical ego experience.

Suppose we decide to remain in the physical or Astral regions firmly attached to our ego identification instead of leading our lives as fully self-realised and self-actualised individuals, lumbering along, unthinkingly confronting our challenges in a state of judgemental partiality, blinded by our emotions and prejudices. In that case, we have a much harder job of learning our lessons and evolving towards and integrating with our authentic selves. On the other hand, if we look at our challenges from an enlightened, non-attached viewpoint, we will quickly grasp the significance and deeper meaning of a challenge in life and are equipped to deal with it efficiently, wisely and objectively. Burdened with our ego, it is like saying: "If I want to be of help in the world, I have to be plagued by arthritis, blindness and with one hand tied behind my back". This experience may have been lacking until now, but it won't help us on the path towards integration and felt realisation. The ego by itself will bind us into a perpetual state of imprisonment. How much more enjoyable are the events of our planet when our mind is at peace and in a state of liberation? Our heart is humming with joy, wisdom and inspiration from our unity self,

The shrine of the divine light

The Divine Light

141 *Elysium Unveiled*

Realms of Light

knowing that we are already home and our task at hand is one of true compassionate service towards ourselves and others, not one of obligation, confusion and pain.

Yes, it is true; heaven is here, and it is now, and we don't have to die to enter it, and if we reach our true state after we die, there is nothing in the world that can prevent us from entering the Astral or the physical world again and carry on living there in a state of peace and stillness with our heart brimming with love and joy.

This book is about states of consciousness and their corresponding environments. We have already seen so far throughout this book how our state of consciousness determines our experience and the environment we find ourselves in, as well as the energy, or lack of it, which is accessible to us the more our ego identification gives way to the power of love and wisdom, released by our true self of Unity Consciousness. So what will our corresponding world and environment look like to us when we are no longer tied to the entanglements of our cosmic web, the total of our past experiences, conflicts, incarnations and attachments?

143 Elysium Unveiled

Realms of Beauty and Symmetry

Books have been written about the awakening process taking place while we are still incarnate here on earth, anchored to the physical world around us with our senses conditioned and programmed by our sensory experience and perception. But what about when we are no longer here in this material world? When our consciousness is no longer bound by our physical perceptions? What if we finally realise while out of our body either through death or an Out-of-Body experience? What will we see and encounter?

There are as many ways of transcending our limited and conditioned ego state as people living on Earth, and each one of us will have our own unique experiences. There are not many such visceral reports of such a transition taking place in the non-physical state, and I can only speak of my own.

I had several experiences, and each one was different, from being confronted by a vast and glorious Gate of Heaven, allowing only a glimpse

The many mansions of Heaven

145 Elysium Unveiled

Realms of Creation

through it into the other side, to passing through the proverbial "Portals of Heaven" into the state of Unity Consciousness. I already documented in my first book a spontaneous peak experience that opened the gates for me and blessed me with the siddhi of OBE for the rest of my life and all I documented. I also reported a great tower with a winding staircase. Two mighty warrior angels guarding the entrance. I ascended the stairs to the top and met my brother, who later too realised his authentic state of being. In every case of transcendence, it was always towards the light, the essence of our being, our Unity Consciousness or even God. These experiences and many others happened while my awareness was no longer focused on the physical experience but on the ineffable state of heightened OBE. But it doesn't have to be. It can also be an in-between state. One time, I was sitting in meditation and gazing with my inner eye through a transparent membrane, where I found my authentic self waiting for me on the far side, enticing my awareness to join it, which I then did and merged with my authentic true self in a somewhat unexceptional manner. At other times, I was gripped in mid-conversation, in mid-sentence and catapulted into a state of sublime unity consciousness, without interrupting for a second of what I was

A guide will be at hand to take us across the great divides

And when you feel you have reached the top of these worlds, the heavens open, inviting you to claim higher glories.

147 Elysium Unveiled

Realms of Creation

saying and without anybody in the room noticing anything at all. All this is to serve as documentation that we already are our natural Unity Consciousness on a temporary trip into a lower state of awareness. This is different when out of the body.

From Christian mystics, we find descriptions of a "Heaven's Gate", which are powerful metaphors they use to describe a transition from one state of awareness to another which is so different and so glorious that human language and our knowing mind is challenged to its limit to find words for it. So why is it such a challenge, and why do we know so little about it?

Because we are dealing with altered states of consciousness, which are completely beyond what our everyday awareness is used to. If we have finally established our awareness in a state of Unity Consciousness as a result of lifetime meditation or spiritual practice, integrated it into our day-to-day living where we live every moment in the presence of the divine, the Here and Now that assures our permanently connection with our divine core, then we live constantly in a feeling of being "Home" no matter where we are.

When in this state, after having left our physical shell and grown accustomed to what it means to be living in a very fluid state of

Once we enter these higher states, the sense of fulfilment and joy is overflowing.

Entering the high states of Unity Consciousness grants divine wisdom, knowledge, unlimited freedom, and unconditional love. Those who attain this state will not have to reincarnate unless they choose to do so.

However, it is important to note that this is just the beginning of our true life.

Realms of Unconditional Love

consciousness, our three-dimensional Earth and its gravity no longer dictate our experience and perception. The old conditionings and habits, even the conditions of Astral life have become redundant in favour of a more bliss-inducing fluidity. This is brought about by the flow of much finer creative energies which can mould and respond instantly to our will, in harmony with a much greater divine will, integrated and interwoven with a cosmic kind of awareness. This gives our life an entirely new meaning, totally incomparable with our life of old.

So this transition within the non-physical from one state into divine life may lead us through such a gateway. This is comparable to a similar experience of passing through a tunnel often reported by people with near-death experiences, which signifies the transition of the physical consciousness into the Astral. Here, we are already in the fluid state of the Astral, and our transition into a new state of consciousness is often signified by the metaphor of passing through a gate, which can take on many forms. The appearance of the gate, or its "design," is entirely dictated by the individual energy of the person passing through it, and every pass-through will be different, as I have observed, every time I entered this higher state, but every time we are assured of a grand and extraordinary new entry. It can even be a glorified and quite bliss inducing passage through a kaleidoscope wormhole. (People with access to a VR headset can get an impression of what it feels like by trying a few apps I created and posted on my website.)

This is indeed an extraordinary event, acknowledged and celebrated by a spiritual hierarchy and community already firmly established in the place we will recognise as your true home.

When we approach the gateway to this magnificent state of our home, we may be completely overwhelmed by its unaccustomed splendour and glory. We will be immediately reminded that something exceptional is about to happen even as we approach it. We may also become aware that our Astral body becomes a burden, like a heavy winter coat we must leave outside when we enter a comfortable and well-heated home. Our old ego attachments have been unmasked as inappropriate, foolish and have no place here. We are done with this awkward, childish old self, which is nothing more than an embarrassment in the face of what is real and true.

If we still cling to the old habits, we will experience discomfort and return to our bodies instead of

Bathing under a waterfall is a download of wisdom and knowledge.

151 *Elysium Unveiled*

Eternal Love

taking the next step. But the moment we recognise where we truly belong and are filled with joy and anticipation of our homecoming, these are no longer any concerns, and we will hardly be able to resist the pull, even if it appears to be tearing us apart. The gate will open, accompanied by an experience of supreme blessing and ecstatic joy.

On one such occasion, I experienced the blessing of flower petals raining down on me from the Heavens above as I passed through. Simultaneously, a heavenly choir of a thousand angelic voices would greet me. I was amazed and overwhelmed that such a fuss was afforded for simple me and garnered the attention of so many souls who had gathered to give me such a welcome. Initially, I dismissed this as a thought form from my unconscious mind. I thought I had materialised it as an angelic choir, but we must not dismiss the significance of such a transition on our collective Unity Consciousness. We know how significant our liberated awareness is for all of life, not just ours. By entering the divine consciousness, we become a coworker with this universal energy, adding a new potency to the divine plan for our human evolution.

What happens when we return to our source, Unity or Cosmic Consciousness? It will be an experience tailored specifically to each individual soul as if you are the only person in existence. This uniquely privileged experience will be the most profound in anybody's life. It would be presumptuous to make any statement about this because it is unique for everyone. This is when the Buddha falls silent, and silence is most likely the most appropriate statement anybody can make about it.

People with only their imagination to visualise what may happen when we unite with our source often presume we will be absorbed, dissolved into a cosmic soup of consciousness, which amounts to nothingness, never to emerge again into the land of the living. Nothing can be further from the truth because the opposite is happening: a unification with all life as one great soul. I think such fantasies are routed in the fact that we don't know and cannot know because our perception and cognitive faculties can not reach beyond what is already known and is way beyond the jurisdiction of the mind.

What we can say is that when our evolution as consciousness unfolds, our freedom expands exponentially and instead of coming to the end of our path, we are only just beginning, born into a new life with astonishing and unimaginable prospects, embarking on a further stairway of much higher celestial evolution. Our consciousness keeps expanding, and at this stage, we cannot even intuit where it will take us except for a feeling of increasing wonder and blessedness.

In my humble experience, documented in my first book, I reported about a supreme clarity with no attributes, an awareness of something absolute, and the many mystics who tried to describe it inevitably failed to find words. At that time, I could not say whether this would be a permanent state or simply a waypoint of recalibration, a reset, which it turned out to be as I ended up being confronted with my fallibilities and feebleness of my human existence when I reemerged out of my ecstasy.

I knew then that I was reborn; my life was reset, but I had been endowed with new awareness, which made me look at everything in a completely new light. If this transition happens to us after death, it is impossible to say what will happen if we don't reenter the physical world as I did back then. Being

When we enter Unity Consciousness we are truly united with our lovers or departed loved ones, because, perhaps for the first time, will we realise true unconditional love and what it means to belong to one source consciousness.

It is here that people sometimes report encounters with God or Divine Entities.

During a retreat in 2021 I met "The Divine Feminine", manifested as a radiant Goddess, during a deep meditation. She was bathed in golden light, surrounded by a tapestry of flowers and she overwhelmed me with her love, which I could still feel weeks later.

Celestial Bliss

liberated means we have freedom of choice and can reside wherever we wish. The numerous helpers populating the astral dimensions and who are only a call away are testimony to this. Once we enter our true state, we become the guides, the angels, the celestial guardians, who are free to choose and work wherever they wish or are sent to by their greater self. We find such helpers on earth in the poorest favelas, refuge camps, and slums. Angels who may not even have any recollection of where they have descended from, but they are here among us.

So we are Bodhisattvas, free to choose; we may wish to enter the Astral world repeatedly and learn and evolve in particular ways.

Liberation means liberation because the whole kingdom of God will be ours to explore rather than dissolve into a Cosmic Soup or be devoured by an all-encompassing nothing Consciousness. For the first time, we will know what true freedom means, where we can decide to enter the lower Astral worlds, including the deepest hells if we so choose, and the highest heavens, endowed with new skill sets and an expanded consciousness whilst being permanently linked to our source powered by its outpouring of love.

So what may it look like? What may we find in these sublime regions? Are there any words for it? To give an analogy in terms of experience, it feels as if everything is supported by a sublime music score, which renders everything sublime. It makes us float rather than walk. We are elevated by the divine intelligence surrounding us. It can be a landscape of light in trillions of colours laid out before us. The air vibrating with sublime harmonies. In this purest state of mind and heart, everything reveals its inner beauty to us and our connectedness. New celestial vistas emerge before our eyes simply because our focus changes. We can create, travel via a shift of focus, visit, experience and even become anything we wish because already we know we are at the root of all.

"I was standing at the edge of an eternal ocean, with mounting waves of light crashing ashore and overwhelming me. With every wave, I experience the ecstasy of being enveloped by love, surrendered in devotion, overwhelmed by gratitude, that I was chosen to be in the presence of an almighty power in charge and at the root of all. "

We may feel a pull via enchanting melodies so intimately known towards an existing colony of like-minded friends or a consensus city strangely familiar to us. Our friends and loved ones are already in the purity of their authentic being, regardless of whether their material awareness is still fastened in some lower realm. But their soul is wide awake here, and we are closer than ever.

Or we may visit the super-dimensional counterpart of a favourite place on Earth and experience it in its sublime essence and splendour. We may visit alien worlds in another universe, their planets made of unknown substances, so strange that we will quickly adopt a new set of sensory perceptions to tune into this world. The surprising thing is that we will experience it as our home, which we have never left.

But let us not be fooled into believing that we have reached an endpoint; it simply does not exist. "Endpoint" is an assumption, an abstraction only applicable to our limited worldview and the mind. In the greater reality, there are no starts or endpoints because one moment flows into the next, carried on the back of a sound, a life current without beginning and end. All of existence flows, transforms, mutates and harmonises.

The pure ultimate state of being is just that, "Being". Nothing moves. It is stillness, in essence, which does not exist when our focus is firmly fixed on the exclusive worlds of thought, intellect and emotions, where we so easily get trapped. It is a stillness with infinite potential, utterly unattached to the world's dramas and in its core state, it has no attributes. We are it. There is no outside world. We become what we encounter. We become what we have always been, the presence of the divine. There is no separateness.

It is impossible to understand why this is so because it simply is. It is everywhere and everything and expresses itself as pure love throughout. We may begin to fathom the great mystery of its core, and wonder whether there may be stillness beyond the stillness and God beyond God, reality beyond reality. How far do we dare to travel, and what if we find the answer?

We are Here Now

For now we are rooted with both feet in the physical world; we have chosen to sort out our "stuff". Our time here is precious because physical existence, with its limitations imposed on us, is vital for our individual learning and spiritual progress. Our lives are restricted. Our time here is precious because it is limited, with opportunities to make the most of it. We can only learn what we imposed on ourselves to learn here on earth. So we do our best to get on with our worldly jobs, not even realising that every hour provides opportunities for individual advancement. When we begin to realise that it is love, appreciation, and compassion which provides the most potent foundation to acquire knowledge and wisdom, we not only achieve our goals here on earth in the best possible way, but we also lay the groundwork for an exhilarating, inspired and rewarding infinite future which stretches before us without limitation.

We begin life in the shadow and rise into the bright sky of eternal light. Our path here will be completed soon enough, and the more work we do here now by acting authentically, truthfully, with integrity, motioned by love, generosity of mind and spirit, we naturally follow the highway to our home, our true home and will be spared the stresses ignorance and selfishness entails.

Our tasks here are often dreary, exhausting and perhaps quite dull. Still, each time, they can remind us to focus on the heart while confronted, and things will instantly become more exciting and rewarding. Our challenges will provide the anchor for reminding us to employ the heart in our daily tasks, and so challenges will become positive triggers for change rather than an annoyance. By fastening our awareness to this very moment, the now with its inherent stillness and its inexhaustible potential, we are already close to our true home. So our conflicts become our servants, anchoring us to the reality of NOW.

It is an illusion to think our life and opportunities for self-expression end when we are done with our issues and our attachments when we enter true reality in enlightenment, our authentic state, our home state. Instead, life only ever unfolds. Life is full of significance and mystery, and we can make it anything we wish. Rooted in the creative outward flow, which is unconditional love, we are free to participate in all creation. We don't waste away in a featureless, empty space, bored out of our wits with some imagined bliss we know little about. We become co-workers with the creator in absolute liberation. We are free to choose how to go about it, where to focus and place our awareness, which group of souls to join and what to do. We are not condemned to sit on some imagined celestial cloud but are liberated to guide, help, participate, and even descend into the depths of darkness like true Bodhisattvas if we wish. We are the co-workers with our source. True happiness lies here and we will never be alone, because we are enveloped in a mantle of divine love.

We can join communities of kindred spirits, cooperate on unimaginable creative projects and visit any part of Infinity we wish for or are called to. We are the working army of absolute consciousness. If you've ever wondered where Angels come from, now you know. We are the Angels. This is how Angels are borne. Emanuel Swedenborg was adamant about it: the armies of angels are no supernatural beings; they were once humans like you and me.

The majesty and splendour of the worlds we can visit have no boundaries. We no longer live in a dimension limited by linear time and space. We are in the world of consciousness, and wherever we are, and whatever we focus on, we are there and are in reality and in a powerful, super awake state of consciousness. We are no longer tied to any specific place; all that is needed is awareness. Awareness is the point zero; from here, all things are possible. The idea that we are in a specific linear place in our evolution is an illusion. There are no stacked levels of states of consciousness as is commonly believed or that consciousness is a linear state of progression involving time and space. These are our three-dimensional illusions. In reality, Truth is right here, right now, where we are, and it only requires a shift in focus to realise.

When I became aware of it, I thought, "How could I have forgotten? How could I ever forget or not be aware of it?" It is right in front of our noses. It is as simple as waking from a dream. Once fully awoken and immersed, it is natural and clear as day. Nothing else is real. Consciousness is all and is everywhere. We are aware, and we are where we focus. We become what we think. There is no longer separation or an outside world divorced from us.

Where do I come from?

157 *Elysium Unveiled*

Evolved Humans

Many years ago, after visiting the purely spiritual regions and observing the inhabitants living there, I exclaimed, being taken aback by the splendour and beauty of the inhabitants, "What an incredibly beautiful species we are." In these regions, people will have dealt with all their ego identification and will have shed them like the heavy burden they are. None has surrendered their individuality; all will have realised much more of their potential, gained in wisdom, experience and beauty. The purity of being in close contact with your divine source means you will have realised a new level of freedom and authenticity. Your inner purity is manifested in your body, and your aura radiates a profound love that elevates everybody who comes in contact with you. Love reigns supreme and is no longer gender related. It no longer matters what gender identity we assume, and only love counts, which provides a closeness between friends which takes your breath away. In 2021, I met my friends from another era during a deep meditation. I was shocked at how close and intimately they were residing in my heart, like nothing I had ever experienced before in my life. If you are lovers, expect an ecstatic intimacy of another dimension. Not only are you finally home where you belong, but you are united with your loved one in a way you cannot even imagine in the Astral Realm.

Rejoice! You are at home, united with your source and loved ones, and from here on, a completely new chapter of your afterlife will emerge.

Every person we meet has their unique and individual aura. We are fully unfolded and self realised and rather than merging into perceived uniformity, the opposite takes place. We rise into our radiant self and for the first time are who we are meant to be all along: radiant diving beings. We are the Angels all religions talk about.

Reincarnation

Over the fifty years of exploring consciousness and its corresponding environments, I was privileged to observe phenomena first-hand, which have either been a matter of belief or speculation. I observed aborted babies being welcomed by the loving hands of new Astral mothers. I watched people reentering a new incarnation from the other side and met babies of friends waiting for their incarnation before my friends even knew they had conceived. I even met my own daughter during one OBE, waiting for her incarnation.

I also visited many of my past lives, where I entered my past life avatars and knew and understood everything they were thinking, their circumstances, their fears and most intimate secrets. I saw myself die during a past life and experienced how I had affected the lives of others. I was privy to observing the incarnation process from a unified consciousness perspective. I learned how we assemble the energy for our next incarnation and how we can liberate ourselves from the continuing cycle of death and rebirth.

Reincarnation is just one other natural process of nature and part of our ongoing evolution unfolding of individual consciousness. We are not separate from the greater consciousness and just cannot make a decision whether we wish to reincarnate or not from our limited ego perspective. For this, we simply do not have the oversight needed because we are intricately linked to other units of consciousness and all our past actions. To make the decision of how and where we wish to incarnate, we, as an individual ego, simply do not have all the information at our disposal to make a wise decision. Fortunately, the greater aspect of ourselves, our Unity consciousness, does. When I entered this state one day, as I was lying on my bed and was whisked away into the core of my being, I could see the whole process at work. I found myself in a giant network of billions of centre points connected to each other. At every connection point, I found another aspect of myself, pertinent information about past actions and experiences and past lives. I could also see how these centre points were connected to each other, and by following them, I could get the information of why and how. I could home my awareness in on any of these billions of points, and I could scoop the information. It is within this giant network of information where our next incarnation is being decided. And it is via a process of attraction and energetic harmonisation. It can be likened to a giant computer, and the greater consciousness or our Soul runs the computer program if you like.

To extract ourselves from this cosmic web, we need to become aware of ourselves of who we are at our core consciousness. When this happens, we become enlightened. Each fibre of who we are, each information centre point, becomes enlightened. Not only that. At that moment, we merge our awareness with the cosmos. When I experienced this on a retreat in Scotland many years ago, I became aware of the suffering and the joy of every living creature. It was harrowing as well as an experience of profound ecstasy.

Each individual person or soul alive is part of this cosmic unity, where we are all united and one, blessed by the creator of all with unconditional love.

– The End –

We are one

We have many lives

161 Elysium Unveiled

Meet the Author: Jurgen Ziewe

Jurgen Ziewe is not your typical author; he is a seeker, an explorer, and a relentless pursuer of truth. Since 1969, he has been following a strict regime of meditation, seeking to unlock the mysteries of consciousness. But it was a moment of sheer serendipity during breakfast that changed everything. In an instant, he experienced a profound dissociation from his physical body, plunging headlong into a realm of absolute clarity. This spontaneous peak experience would mark the beginning of an extraordinary journey.

Rather than resting on this remarkable event, Jurgen continued to delve deeper into his meditation practice, paying homage to the experience with a newfound humility. He soon found himself drawn into a world of spontaneous Out-of-Body experiences that spanned five decades. These experiences, he would later realise, were a direct result of that transformative moment of consciousness singularity.

With hundreds of hours spent in a super-waking awareness during these out-of-body states, Jurgen meticulously mapped out the multidimensional reality that awaits humanity after physical death. Along his journey, he encountered a Chinese Master who initiated him into an intensive training process, guiding him toward elevated states of consciousness.

In 1980, Jurgen experienced another profound state of absolute clarity during one of his OBE journeys. These and other significant encounters were meticulously documented in his diaries and later shared with the world through his books, including "Multidimensional Man" in 2008, "Vistas of Infinity" in 2015, and "The Ten Minute Moment," which chronicled a singular event during a solitary mountain retreat.

Beyond his spiritual pursuits, Jurgen is also a highly successful commercial illustrator, serving clients around the globe. His latest work takes us on a mesmerising journey into the visual landscapes of other-dimensional realities through the medium of Virtual Reality. These experiences are generously offered to the public, allowing others to glimpse the boundless possibilities of these alternate realms.

Jurgen Ziewe sees himself not as a teacher but as a reporter, delivering a down-to-earth narrative of his remarkable experiences. His work has captured the attention of the scientific community, leading to lectures at universities and consciousness conventions.

In his professional life, Jurgen remains a sought-after commercial illustrator, leveraging cutting-edge CG technology used in the film industry and the revolutionary capabilities of AI to vividly document his journeys in alternate realities. His graphic testimonies have drawn comparisons to the works of Swedenborg, offering an unprecedented and deeply detailed exploration of the infinite layers of human consciousness.

In his own words, Jurgen reflects on his extraordinary journey:

"I no longer need to leave my body, although it happens spontaneously. The multidimensional reality to me is like an open book. The moment I close my eyes, I am surrounded by a brilliant field of energy, an open scenery of white light, which tears my heartstrings, and I am instantly at home, my true divine home. I call it the 'Silver World.' Whatever I focus on emerges clearly in my field of vision. I can pick any clue or image and be guided into new and unexpected places. Perhaps it's what all artists do. I am nothing special. I allow the core of my consciousness, my innermost being, to take charge of me. All this happens while blessed with profound love, wrapped up in the realisation that I am one with my divine source."

Please visit:

www.multidimensionalman.com
www.thetenminutemoment.com
www.magicfantasyart.com

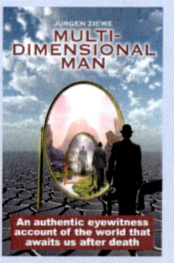 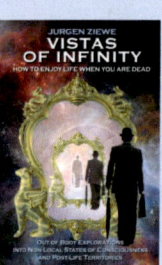 

www.ingramcontent.com/pod-product-compliance
Lightning Source LLC
Chambersburg PA
CBRC101245160426
43209CB00026B/1896